P9-DFN-682

Michel de Ghelderode

Twayne's World Authors Series
French Literature

David O'Connell, Editor
Georgia State University

TWAS 845

Michel de Ghelderode in 1954.

Michel de Ghelderode

David B. Parsell

Furman University

Twayne Publishers ■ New York

Maxwell Macmillan Canada ■ Toronto

Maxwell Macmillan International ■ New York Oxford Singapore Sydney

KNIGHT-CAPRON LIBRARY
LYNCHBURG COLLEGE
LYNCHBURG, VIRGINIA 24501

PQ
2613
.H17
Z82
1993

Michel de Ghelderode
David B. Parsell

Copyright 1993 by Twayne Publishers

All rights reserved. No part of this book may be reproduced or transmitted in any form or by any means, electronic or mechanical, including photocopying, recording, or by any information storage and retrieval system, without permission in writing from the Publisher.

Twayne Publishers   Maxwell Macmillan Canada, Inc.
Macmillan Publishing Company   1200 Eglinton Avenue East
866 Third Avenue   Suite 200
New York, New York 10022   Don Mills, Ontario M3C 3N1

Library of Congress Cataloging-in-Publication Data

Parsell, David B.
    Michel de Ghelderode / David B. Parsell.
    p. cm. – (Twayne's world authors series; TWAS 845)
    Includes bibliographical references and index.
    ISBN 0-8057-4303-0 (alk. paper)
    1. Ghelderode, Michel de, 1898-1962 – Criticism and interpretation. I. Title. II. Series.
PQ2613.H17Z82   1993
848'.91209 – dc20   93-27293
                                                                       CIP

The paper used in this publication meets the minimum requirements of American National Standard for Information Sciences – Permanence of Paper for Printed Library Materials, ANSI Z39.48-1984.

10 9 8 7 6 5 4 3 2 1

Printed in the United States of America.

In memory of Franklin Grant Hamlin

23 June 1915 – 14 January 1990

Department of Romance Languages

Hamilton College

1948-1980

KNIGHT-CAPRON LIBRARY
LYNCHBURG COLLEGE
LYNCHBURG, VIRGINIA 24501

Contents

KNIGHT-CAPRON LIBRARY   vii
LYNCHBURG COLLEGE
LYNCHBURG, VIRGINIA 24501

Preface

Had this study been undertaken a quarter-century earlier, in the aftermath of Michel de Ghelderode's death – by which time an English-language survey of his plays was already somewhat overdue – the result might well have been quite different. As I show and discuss in the following pages, Ghelderode died in the process of being "discovered" outside of Belgium and France by literary and theater professionals alike. His plays, uncommonly resistant to interpretation or classification, were hailed worldwide for their originality, much as they had been in France after World War II. With the passage of time, however, it has become both possible and necessary to view Ghelderode's plays with objectivity and in perspective, avoiding many of the superlatives once applied to his work.

To a great degree, the altered perspective regarding Ghelderode's career is due to the work of Roland Beyen, a Fleming fluent in French, like the playwright himself. Since the late 1960s Beyen has assumed the task of separating fact from fiction perpetuated by Ghelderode and accepted at face value by most of his earlier commentators. Approaching the study of Ghelderode's plays with methods appropriate to a literary historian and critic, Beyen soon discovered gaping discrepancies between public statement and recorded evidence, not only with regard to Ghelderode's life but also, and initially, regarding the composition of his plays. In the light of Beyen's subsequent discoveries, much early work on Ghelderode stands in need of revision, and students of Ghelderode ignore Beyen's research at their peril. Unfortunately, the work of Beyen and his colleagues remains unavailable in English, as do many of the better early studies.

Rich in sight, sound, and presumably imagined smells, the best of Ghelderode's plays continue to tempt "theatricians" (the term is Ruby Cohn's) the world over, promising truly spectacular possibilities seldom even approached in the work of other recent dramatists. With time, however, it has become increasingly difficult to dismiss or "explain" the ill-concealed misogyny and ethnic prejudices that

often loom so large in Ghelderode's plays that they are instrumental
to the plot. In an age quite justifiably, if at times obsessively, concerned with "inclusive language" and "multiculturalism,"
Ghelderode's plays remain quite resolutely "exclusive" and
"incorrect," deliberately harking back to the Middle Ages and early
Renaissance when sexual and ethnic stereotypes were used, however
inadvertently, to provide "civilization" with its "structure."

Tempting though it might be to "excuse" Ghelderode's recourse
to stereotype as yet another theatrical device, biographical evidence
brought to light by Beyen and his successors suggests otherwise.
What is more, it is nearly impossible to adapt or "launder"
Ghelderode's theatrical expression in order to make it more accept-
able to socially sensitive audiences. Ghelderode thus remains, as
Lionel Abel described him, "our man in the sixteenth century,"
writing in a distinctly modern style and idiom from voluntary exile in
another time. His contribution to world drama, however incon-
testable, is therefore problematic some three decades after his death.

Work on this study was begun in the late 1980s, by which time
Roland Beyen had permanently altered the course of Ghelderode
studies, recently augmented by Jacqueline Blancart-Cassou's investi-
gation and analysis of laughter in Ghelderode's theatrical universe, a
study embracing the author's entire life and career. Also available
were the proceeds of two international conferences devoted exclusively to Ghelderode and his work held in 1978 and 1982.

Although Ghelderode's published work includes poetry (most of
it pseudonymous), short fiction, and nonfiction, it is as a dramatist
that he established his reputation and is most likely to be remembered. His nondramatic work, moreover, remains unavailable in
English and is of interest mainly for the light that it sheds (or does
not shed) on the development and process of his playwriting. For
that reason I focus primarily on the plays in this study, emphasizing
those texts most widely disseminated in Great Britain and in North
America. Readers and theatricians fluent in French are referred to
the Bibliography, where I have made every effort to select and call
attention to the strongest and most pertinent commentaries.

To Furman University, I am grateful for institutional support for
the preparation of this volume, including a Charles A. Dana grant
during the summer of 1988 for the research and bibliographical ser-
vices of Mr. Kevin Smith, then a Furman undergraduate. I am grateful

also to Kevin himself, as to Mrs. Carolyn Sims, whose typing and proofreading, as usual, go well above and beyond the call of duty. Thanks also to my wife, Sharon, daughter, Margaret and son, John, for their patience; thanks most of all to Professor Frank Hamlin, who first opened my eyes and ears to the possibilities of French theater, and to whose memory this volume is dedicated.

Chronology

1898	Adémar-Adolphe-Louis Martens, later to style himself Michel de Ghelderode, born 3 April (Palm Sunday) in Ixelles, Belgium.
1906	Begins schooling at the Institut Saint-Louis in Brussels.
1914	Studies are cut short by a near fatal attack of typhus.
1915-1917	Studies music (viola) at the Royal Conservatory of Music and is subsequently employed as an arts critic for a business weekly.
1918	First play, *La Mort regarde à la fenêtre*, signed "Ghelderode," performed 29 April.
1919-1921	Performs military service, which had been postponed owing to illness and convalescence; writes poetry and short fiction while in uniform.
1921	Returns to civilian life and accepts teaching post from which he soon resigns owing to precarious health.
1922	In August is hired by Lebègue bookstore, where he meets his future wife, Jeanne-Françoise Gérard.
1923	In April is hired as clerk by the Commune of Schaarbeek, where he will remain employed for more than 20 years.
1924	Marries Jeanne-Françoise Gérard in civil ceremony in February; in October publishes poetry attributed to "Philostène Costenoble"; releases first of "restored" puppet plays in November.
1925	*La Mort du Docteur Faust* performed (published in 1926).

1926	"Discovered" and engaged by Vlaamsche Volkstoon-neel (VVT), or the Flemish Popular Theater; *Images de la vie de Saint Francois d'Assise*; begins *Don Juan*.
1927	*Christophe Colomb*; *Escurial*.
1928	*Barabbas*.
1929	*Pantagleize*.
1930	Dissension within VVT. Martens legally changes name to Ghelderode in July. Actor Renaat Verheyen, inter-preter of the Ghelderode characters Saint Francis and Pantagleize, dies in October.
1931	Ghelderode begins writing plays more and more "for himself," returning to medieval/Renaissance setting for themes and inspiration. *Magie rouge*.
1932	Final collapse of VVT; Ghelderode now on his own.
1933	*Le Siège d'Ostende*.
1934	*Sire Halewyn*; *La Balade du grand macabre*.
1935	*Mademoiselle Jaire*; *Sortie de l'acteur* completed.
1936	*D'un diable qui prêcha merveilles*; *La Farce des ténébreux*; *Hop, Signor!*
1937	*Fastes d'enfer*.
1939-1940	Returns to short fiction, composing the tales to be collected in *Sortilèges*.
1941	Begins writing and reading broadcast "column" for Radio-Brussels, now under Nazi occupation.
1942	*L'Ecole des bouffons*.
1943	*Le Soleil se couche*.
1945-1946	Accused of collaboration with the Nazis, Ghelderode is relieved of his bureaucratic post and works hard toward reinstatement, taking retirement pension instead. First indications of Parisian interest in the staging of his plays.

1947-1953   Ghelderode's plays belatedly "discovered" by Parisian actors, directors, and theatergoers. First performances of *Fastes d'enfer* cause scandal late in 1949; "Acute Ghelderoditis" diagnosed by journalist Guy Dornand early in 1950, soon after which the Paris-based publishing house of Gallimard begins issuing Ghelderode's plays in a standard, multivolume edition.

1951   Taping and broadcast of the Ostend Interviews.

1952   *Marie la misérable* prepared on commission.

1952-1962   Ghelderode's fame begins to spread outside of France and Belgium, inspiring numerous translations and productions of his plays.

1962   Ghelderode dies on 1 April while under consideration for year's Nobel Prize for Literature.

Chapter One

"Our Man in the Sixteenth Century": The Lives and Times of Ghelderode

Sure at last of a receptive audience and evoking a childhood by then recalled as solitary, Michel de Ghelderode wondered aloud in 1951 in the now-famous *Entretiens d'Ostende* (or Ostend Interviews) if he might not, indeed, have been born onto the wrong planet.[1] Barely a dozen years later, after Ghelderode's death, the American critic Lionel Abel would present the enigmatic, reclusive Belgian playwright as "Our Man in the Sixteenth Century," coining a trite but appropriate phrase that Ghelderode himself, given his penchant for mystification, would no doubt have appreciated and enjoyed.[2] To be sure, Ghelderode liked to envision himself as a lone artist adrift in time and space; still, no appreciation of the man or his work can be complete without some understanding of the time and place that formed his character and talent.

Despite his intense preoccupation with the past, both European and specifically Belgian, the playwright Ghelderode belongs very much to his own time, roughly the first half of the twentieth century. Although too young to serve in World War I at its outset and subsequently incapacitated by a near-fatal case of typhus that kept him out of uniform until after the 1918 Armistice, Ghelderode fully qualifies as "our man" in Abel's memorable phrase. Formed in the climate of the Great War and its aftermath, Ghelderode's artistic consciousness emerges as fully modern, at times postmodern, even as his portrayals of human nature tend to seek, and find, the timeless and the universal. On the negative side, Ghelderode shares also in the unexamined prejudices of his time; to later generations even the strongest of his dramatic efforts raise serious questions of racism and sexism that cannot easily be dismissed.

It is with regard to place, however, that Ghelderode's art remains most fully "determined" and hence, ironically, most difficult to classify. Like the Belgian nation itself in microcosm, Ghelderode's drama is a cultural phenomenon seriously, almost irreconcilably, divided against itself by a barrier of language. Writing always in French, the Flemish Ghelderode achieved his first successes in the theater through Dutch translations prepared by other hands. When at last, some two decades later, his plays were widely performed in their original French, they proved difficult, if not impossible, for the French audience to appreciate or even understand, irreducibly "foreign" in tone and content despite the author's flawless, often beautiful command of the French idiom. Ironically, Ghelderode's temporal and spatial roots often seemed to conspire against him. When, at 53, he dramatically questioned his choice of planet before an appreciative radio audience, he was no doubt indulging in a bit of wishful thinking.

Birth and Childhood

The individual later to style himself Michel de Ghelderode was born on Palm Sunday, 3 April 1898, in Ixelles, a suburb of Brussels frequented by artists and writers. His name, formalized at baptism two weeks later, was Adémar-Adolphe-Louis Martens. Known as Adolphe within the family, the future playwright was the third son and youngest child born to Henri-Alphonse Martens (1861-1943), employed at the Royal Archives, and the former Jeanne-Marie Rans (1864-1944), who had once planned to become a nun and who had later served, against her husband's wishes, as proprietress of a café. According to Ghelderode, who often played fast and loose with fact, Henri-Alphonse had dissuaded Jeanne-Marie from her religious vocation by the simple expedient of pregnancy. The record does show, in any case, that the author's eldest brother, Marcel, was born within six months following their parents' marriage in January 1889.[3]

Since Ghelderode's death in 1962 his recollections – recorded in the Interviews and elsewhere – have come under serious scrutiny by scholars, most notably Roland Beyen and Jacqueline Blancart-Cassou, seeking to discover biographical sources for his plays. A number of discrepancies have been discovered. Both scholars, for example, interviewed the author's only sister, Mme Germaine Rucquois, three years Adolphe's senior, who recalled her brother's childhood as normal, far from solitary, perhaps even "happy" (Beyen 1971, 72). Germaine cannot, however, have seen inside her sibling's mind, and there are strong indications that Ghelderode's brooding temperament developed early, together with a fondness for mystification and an enhanced awareness of mortality. Around the age of six, for example, the boy fell ill with a mysterious ailment sufficiently severe that he was sent off to recuperate in a sanatorium on the Belgian coast at Middelkerke – his "exile" lasting, despite the family's modest means, for approximately one year. Not long thereafter the schoolboy Adolphe is said to have "hoaxed" his own suicide, leaving his shoes by a riverbank and hiding in the bushes, waiting for local authorities to discover his evidence and sound the alarm.[4]

There is little doubt, in any case, that Ghelderode grew up closer to his mother than to his father, who favored the two middle children, Ernest and Germaine, perhaps because they most physically resembled him. Almost by default, the eldest, Marcel, and the youngest, Adolphe, sought comfort from the mystical, even superstitious Jeanne-Marie. Adolphe supposedly became suspicious about his ancestry because his father often accused his mother of having committed adultery during a brief return visit to her hometown just nine months before Adolphe's birth (see Blancart-Cassou, 15-17). Significantly, however, when the mature playwright, having already rejected the name Martens in favor of "Ghelderode," attempted to trace his ancestry, he did so through the paternal line (Blancart-Cassou, 16).

Although both native speakers of Dutch, Henri-Alphonse and Jeanne-Marie saw fit to rear and educate their four children as speakers of French, presumably to prepare them for a better future. Until 1888, the year preceding their marriage and Marcel's birth, French had been the only "official" Belgian language, despite a strong majority of Belgians who spoke Flemish, now recognized and known as Dutch. The first literature recognized as Belgian had been written in the French idiom, in part because French was accessible to a wider readership. Maurice Maeterlinck (1862-1949), poet and playwright, typical of the emergent Flemish intelligentsia, wrote exclusively in French and lived mainly in France from his late twenties onward. Although the recognition of Dutch as the second, later the first, official language of Belgium would strongly influence the development of that country's culture during the century to follow, and would loom large in Ghelderode's literary career, the Martens family made what seemed a logical, if upwardly mobile, choice. Ghelderode, as he matured, would use Dutch only in speaking to or about his mother, and there is strong evidence that he never mastered the Dutch language in its written forms (see Beyen 1971, 430-38).

As soon as he was old enough, Ghelderode was sent, as were his brothers, to the nearby Institut Saint-Louis in Brussels for his formal education. Catholic but not Jesuit in affiliation – Ghelderode would later refer to his teachers as *"les messieurs-prêtres"* (the gentlemen-priests), the school offered superior courses in French composition, the only subject in which the future dramatist consistently excelled. For the first six years of his schooling Adolphe lived with his family in the home of his father's boss, where both parents served in effect as household help – a curious arrangement to be sure, and one that ended only with the death of the boss, run over by a streetcar while attempting to watch a solar eclipse (Blancart-Cassou, 15n).

At Saint-Louis, indeed, the mature author's recalled solitude became a matter of fact: Adolphe sought or made few or no friends – on one occasion vigorously resisting the priests' efforts to impose a "friend" on him. The priests, meanwhile, suspected hopefully that the boy's solitary nature might conceal an incipient religious vocation, which it apparently did not. At best indifferent in matters of religion, the boy would "lose his faith" only after the serious attack of typhus that nearly cost him his life at 16, and that effectively ended his formal education.

Toward the end of 1914, still too young to serve in the war that had recently broken out, Adémar-Adolphe Martens fell ill and nearly died of typhus, experiencing what researchers of a later time might well have classified as a "near-death experience." Forever after his quite unexpected recovery, Ghelderode would vividly recall his vision of "a Lady" – possibly the Virgin Mary – who appeared at his bedside to utter the words, "Not now, sixty-three."[5] (As it happened, Ghelderode would die in 1962, just two days short of his sixty-fourth birthday.) It is at this point that Ghelderode would later claim to have lost his faith, primarily because he felt that the priests of his acquaintance were of little help to him during his illness and convalescence (see Blancart-Cassou, 20-21). Arguably, what he lost was his confidence in priests, who would become the frequent objects of satirical wit in his plays. In any event, given the close association of priests and schooling in his life, Adolphe would never return to school – at Saint-Louis or anywhere else – unless one is to count as education the "musical interlude" that followed not long thereafter.

During his fifties, in the Interviews and elsewhere, Ghelderode would recall studying music and even playing string accompaniment to the early silent films. Roland Beyen, researching the matter with his usual close attention to detail, discovered that Adolphe's musical studies were quite minimal, of interest mainly for their association with his discovery of the opposite sex. Beyen does concede, however, that Adolphe's exposure to music might well have trained his ears toward the effective use of sound and melody on the stage (Beyen 1971, 101-109).

Bohemian Beginnings: In Search of "Ghelderode"

In October 1915, less than a year after his illness and recovery, the youth soon to be known as Ghelderode enrolled as a viola student at the Royal Conservatory of Music in Brussels. There is no prior evidence of any latent interest in music on his part, and indeed his "flirtation" with music appears to have been bound up with his flirtation with one Marie van Echel, a neighbor and aspirant musician some 15 months Adolphe's senior. Known variously as Mariette (in French) or Mieke (in Dutch), the young woman appears to have interested her young admirer not only in music but also in her morbid fantasies: the two liked to walk through cemeteries in the rain, or to meet in a hallway that reeked of rotting potatoes, a smell that reminded both of burial and death. In any case, Adolphe's interest in Mariette somewhat outlasted his interest in music. Despite a promising start, Adolphe Martens was dropped from the rolls of the conservatory early in 1917 for infrequent attendance. Mariette, meanwhile, continued to occupy both his time and his thoughts. After a particularly bitter quarrel with her mother, the troubled young woman invited Adolphe to join her in a suicide pact. Meeting in an artist's studio, the two young lovers turned on the gas and waited for death, their wait interrupted every few minutes by the need to drop coins into the gas meter. Perhaps predictably, the couple ran out of change before the gas could kill them, although both fell seriously ill.

A definitive rupture occurred between them not long thereafter: Mariette, by then a professional musician performing in nightclubs and elsewhere, had acquired a rich benefactor/lover who offered to "keep" her. Informing young Martens of this fact, she implied that it would make little difference in their relationship, and that she planned to go on "seeing" him as before. Adolphe, in a sudden access of prudery, replied that he would have no part of such a scheme, denouncing his former friend and mistress as a prostitute. Mariette, haunted as ever by the specter of death, went on with her musical career, dying at 31 of tuberculosis after an incident in which she playfully dared a cabaret customer to drop ice cubes down her back, inducing what turned out to be a fatal chill.[6]

Significantly, the future playwright had taken up with Mariette very shortly after his own close brush with death; without reading too much between the lines, it is possible to see how her morbid fascinations might have fed, and fed upon, his own, helping to develop the artistic consciousness that was soon to emerge. Her musical career, in turn, appears to have opened Ghelderode's ears to the world of sound. Although never a professional musician to the extent that he might have claimed or recalled, Ghelderode nonetheless seems to have acquired, with Mariette's help, sufficient musical literacy to appreciate, judge, and predict the effects of sound and music in the theater.

Even as he courted Mariette and dabbled in music, Adémar-Adolphe Martens was also beginning to try his hand at writing, initially for his own amusement. During the fall of 1917 he sought and found employment as French tutor to the son of a prominent Jewish family from Vienna, the Abramsons, then residing in Brussels; he also encouraged the literary ambitions of the Abramsons' adolescent housekeeper who, years later and with Ghelderode's help, would become a published author under her married name of Madeleine Gevers (Beyen 1971, 109-10). In a classic "bohemian" pattern perhaps more reminiscent of earlier centuries than typical of his own, the young tutor soon began to expend an increasing share of his time and wages in the literary and artistic cabarets of Brussels, gradually drifting into cultural journalism as arts columnist for a financial weekly, *Mercredi-Bourse*. Notable for his eccentricities of speech and dress, the young man was no doubt assumed to be a writer before he had actually written much of anything. Unlike many similar poseurs, however, the emergent Michel de Ghelderode possessed both the determination and the talent to deliver on the promise of his personality.

At the end of April 1918, with the Great War still in progress, the patrons of one of Ghelderode's favorite haunts would witness the initial – and final – performance of his first dramatic effort, already signed with the assumed name of Ghelderode. *La Mort regarde à la fenêtre* (Death Looks in at the Window), appended as if by way of illustration to the young writer's lecture on the life and works of Edgar Allan Poe, could hardly have been written by anyone else, despite its derivations from Poe. The history of the play remains somewhat unclear, blurred by conflicting recollections of Ghelderode and his contemporaries. It might well have been assumed, for example, that the aspiring young man of letters already had a ready supply of play scripts in his portfolio, when in fact he had to start from scratch; it is also possible, though hardly certain, that Ghelderode needed or requested coaching on how to write a play. In any case the text that emerged, deliberately haunted by the shade of Poe, also foreshadowed a number of the mature Ghelderode's dramatic themes and techniques. Notwithstanding, Ghelderode later would all but repudiate his initial attempt at play-writing, refusing ever to include it among his published works (Beyen 1971, 114-18).

As an habitué of Brussels's artistic nightlife, the newly self-styled Michel de Ghelderode would soon befriend, or be befriended by, a number of artists and writers – most of them older; some well-established, others not. Among the better-known figures drawn to Ghelderode by his evident talent and promise was the aging novelist Georges Eekhoud (1854-1927), a pioneer of Belgian literature in French, whose penchant for the odd and the grotesque meshed neatly with the young playwright's developing vision (see Beyen 1971, 119-25). According to Ghelderode, it was Eekhoud who first introduced him to the puppet shows in the Marolles section of Brussels – spectacles that had changed little in form or in content over the preceding centuries. In later years, particularly in the Interviews, Ghelderode would credit the novelist with much of his artistic development, including his growing fondness for Elizabethan theater.

Roland Beyen, carefully tracing Ghelderode's artistic growth, suggests that the dramatist may well, in middle age, have tended to exaggerate his acknowledged debt to Eekhoud for a variety of reasons, not least to discredit what Beyen sees as an even stronger influence, that of a minor writer and graphic artist best known (if at all) as Julien Deladoès. (Born Charles-Julien van der Does during 1886, Ghelderode's supposed mentor spelled his name in a variety of ways for the first 70 years of his long life; known variously as Ladoès, Doës or Does, he also affected the Anglophone pseudonym of William Moore.) According to Beyen, it was Deladoès, far more than Eekhoud, who fed Ghelderode's growing interest in his Flemish heritage. As a connoisseur and collector of art, he also no doubt interested the younger writer in the plastic arts, particularly the works of Bosch and Brueghel the Elder and of the contemporary Belgian artist James Ensor (1860-1949). Unfortunately, Deladoès's own work, which had never fully transcended the decadence of the late nineteenth century, was soon outshone and overshadowed by that of his protégé. In any event, the two men quarreled definitively around 1932, with Ghelderode believing for the remaining three decades of his life that Deladoès had attacked his writings with a campaign of anonymous letters. As a result, suggests Beyen, Ghelderode in his fifties might well have stressed the role of Eekhoud in his career in part to play down that of Deladoès, who would in fact survive him (see Beyen 1971, 125-40).

Another possible influence on Ghelderode's developing sensibilities was that of the mature, married Frenchwoman who became Ghelderode's mistress after his definitive rupture with the doomed Mariette van Echel. Known only as "Madame d'octobre" (the October Lady) after a novel that Ghelderode once planned to write about her, the new love of his life was fully twice his age, well-traveled, cultured and refined. According to Jean Francis, Madame d'octobre assumed a dominant role in Ghelderode's cultural formation, enlarging the scope of his reading and otherwise "deprovincializing" him (Francis, 102-104). Beyen, by contrast, tends to question the extent of the woman's contributions, again citing the tendency of the mature Ghelderode toward selectivity and exaggeration in his recollections. There is, however, little doubt that such a woman did exist and that she served as attentive reader to some of Ghelderode's early writings during a relationship that lasted nearly two years. By the time Madame d'octobre moved on, early in 1919, Ghelderode had acquired a third mistress, a Hungarian known only as Zzalay, with whom he dallied briefly before signing up for his required stint in the military (see Beyen 1971, 140-44).

Like France, Belgium requires military service of all male citizens, usually around age 20. Ghelderode's "class," due to be called in 1918, found conscription deferred by the Armistice until the following spring. Ghelderode, still known officially as A.-A. Martens, enlisted several weeks in advance of his scheduled draft. According to Beyen, he may or may not have sought further deferment for reasons of health, but in the end decided to join up and get it over with. With the war now ended, military service cannot have been challenging; in any case, Ghelderode began his service in the army and ended it, nearly two years later, in the navy, after a tour of duty that would have its American equivalent in the Coast Guard.

As Ghelderode grew older, Beyen observes, his period of military service, like his affair with Madame d' octobre, would loom large in his recollections, subject to occasional exaggeration. At times, he would allude to having been a career sailor, even a merchant seaman, when in fact his assigned vessel seldom, if ever, left the home coast (Beyen 1971, 144-50). When he enlisted, the budding writer was obviously in search of new material, as he confided to Deladoès and other correspondents. Notwithstanding, the stories later collected under the title *L'Homme sous l'uniforme* (The Man under the Uniform) deal less with the implied subject than with a young man's coming of age. Jacqueline Blancart-Cassou finds in several of the tales strong evidence of Ghelderode's ambivalent attitude toward women, later reflected in his plays. Owing in part to his having been "his mother's child," Ghelderode in his earliest short fiction would tend to value maternal or quasi-maternal love over romantic or physical love. One story in particular, "La Passante" (She Who Passes By), appears to have been modeled on his May-December affair with Madame d'octobre" (see Blancart-Cassou, 19-20).

Demobilized in 1921 for reasons of poor health, Ghelderode worked hard at a variety of odd, ill-paying jobs before securing a teaching job for the 1921-22 academic year. Once again, however, frail health intervened, and he was forced to resign his position at mid-year. After six months of joblessness and near destitution, the young veteran was hired during August 1922 as a clerk with the firm of Lebègue, retailers of school supplies, religious articles, and textbooks. It was there that he met his future wife, Jeanne-Françoise Gérard, employed as a bookkeeper.

Three and a half years older than Ghelderode, Jeanne Gérard appears to have been considerably more stable of temperament than her known predecessors in Ghelderode's amatory life. Being older, she may also have satisfied what Blancart-Cassou (23) perceives as Ghelderode's latent need for mothering. Married 2 February 1924 in a civil ceremony, the couple would remain together, although childless, for the rest of Ghelderode's life. As Ghelderode's fame grew, Jeanne would act as his protectress and even watchdog, shielding him from importunate strangers as well as from many mundane details of daily life. Even after Ghelderode's death, Jeanne would remain fiercely protective of his reputation, breaking with Roland Beyen after Beyen had dared to mention in his biography both Deladoès and Ghelderode's sister Germaine; for Jeanne, those people had long since ceased to exist.[7]

Significantly, marriage was not the only change Jeanne Gérard would bring to Ghelderode's life. It was during the period of their engagement, and with Jeanne's connections, that Ghelderode at last obtained stable employment. In April 1923 he joined the bureaucracy of the Brussels Commune of Schaarbeek (where two of his future brothers-in-law already worked), incidentally doubling the salary that he had been earning at Lebègue (Beyen 1971, 155). In a sense, it is ironic that Ghelderode, the son of an even lesser bureaucrat, should find himself in such a dead-end job – a type of work often satirized by such writers as Guy de Maupassant (1850-93) and Marcel Aymé (1902-67). Still, the position of municipal clerk (with increasingly arcane and inconsequential duties) suited both the young man's literary aspirations and his need for creative privacy. Alone in his attic office with few pressing concerns, assured of a steady if modest income, he was able to write in peace, invariably on office letterhead stationery. More than once, his colleagues would take their revenge on such blatant insolence – and indolence – by hanging Ghelderode's latest galley proofs for use as toilet paper in the office lavatory. The increasingly successful author, for his part, was so jealous of his privacy and freedom that he would go for years with a broken skylight in his office, catching leaks with a tin can rather than call attention to himself – or to his writing done on the job – by asking that the window be replaced (Beyen, 1971, 298-300).

From the early 1920s until the end of World War II, Ghelderode was thus able to support himself, and Jeanne, while writing as prolifically as his ambition required, or his health would permit. Under such conditions, both his fiction and his plays began to develop without interruption or impediment, increasingly noticed and appreciated in the cabarets where he had formed his first literary friendships before joining the army. By 1924, the year of his marriage, Ghelderode had already acquired a number of memberships and offices in literary and artistic clubs, respected both for his creative efforts and for his occasional printed reviews. Several of his stories had already been published, and before long he was writing as if compulsively – a fact that may or may not explain the perpetration of his first literary hoax.

It was during 1924 that Ghelderode first invented the persona and works of one Philostène Costenoble, ostensibly an undertaker of his acquaintance who loved literature but did not know how to get his writings published. For years, Ghelderode would insist that the undertaker was quite real and, when pressed, hire an actor to impersonate him. As late as 1947 the playwright claimed to have visited and interviewed Costenoble on the occasion of the latter's sixtieth birthday. In Beyen's view, the Costenoble hoax might well have served Ghelderode as an outlet for works and ideas that he knew to be second rate, or at least beneath his personal standard of quality. By attributing such lesser output to the fictional mortician, he would thus remain free to seek and find a more serious audience for his stronger, more deliberate efforts (Beyen 1971, 167-74). In any event, it is worth noting that "Costenoble" published mainly poetry, a genre normally avoided by Ghelderode when writing under his own (assumed) name.

It is most likely that Ghelderode simply enjoyed the sustained hoax on its own merits, as a kind of game. Not long thereafter he would present a collection of marionette plays ostensibly "restored," using the folklorists' method, from ancient spectacles still being performed in the Marolles district. Subsequent analysis of the texts by Beyen and others would reveal them to be Ghelderode's own work, marked with distinctly modern perspectives and technique. Around the same time Ghelderode also helped to perpetrate a "reverse hoax" of sorts, promoting a mediocre pornographic novel and its hapless author in such a manner as to suggest that he, Ghelderode, might have written the book himself, as was surely true in the case of Costenoble (Beyen 1971, 174-77; see also Blancart-Cassou, 35). In any case, by his mid-twenties Ghelderode was writing with extreme speed, versatility, and skill; recognition would soon follow.

Starting in late adolescence the emergent Ghelderode had been writing both stories and plays, unable or unwilling to choose between genres. By 1925, at least for his "serious" writing, he had begun to shift his attentions almost exclusively toward dramatic texts, publishing his "plays," including the puppet shows, in literary magazines without any apparent expectation that they might ever be performed. For the rest of his active life Ghelderode would in fact tend to write plays "for himself" or for readers, paying little heed to established dramatic conventions. He would also, despite his growing Flemish consciousness, raise his French expression to rare heights of eloquence and aptness. His developing career was thus strangely divided against itself from the start, raising serious questions of which audience he was writing for.

Although he wrote "for himself," Ghelderode, like most aspiring writers, tended to thrive on recognition. As his plays began to gain acceptance among readers he began to push for their performance. As Beyen points out, however, the French-language theater of 1920s Brussels was resolutely conventional, commercial, and crowd-pleasing, similar in spirit to the Paris Boulevard or to New York's Broadway. Avant-garde theater simply did not exist in Brussels, at least not in French, and as a result Ghelderode's increasingly well-known texts appeared destined to remain "homeless" (Beyen 1971, 194-95). It is hardly surprising, therefore, that Ghelderode around 1926 accepted an offer to write plays for the increasingly acclaimed Vlaamsche Volkstoonneel (VVT), or Flemish Popular Theater, regardless of the fact that his efforts would have to be performed in Dutch translations prepared by others more skilled in that language than himself. Indeed, few young (or even older) dramatists would turn down such a ready outlet for their plays, and Ghelderode was no exception.

Ghelderode and the Flemish Popular Theater

Drawn to Ghelderode's works by their author's intense concern with Flemish folklore and culture, the animators of the Flemish Popular Theater (VVT) were in search of new material for their artistically adventurous, increasingly well-received productions. Ghelderode, in turn, was just beginning to be known outside the cabaret circle that had spawned his talent, and an artistic collaboration such as that now offered would afford him the further exposure he sought. At first Ghelderode would turn aside from his "own" work-in-progress, such as *Don Juan*, to furnish requested plays on demand; in time, however, with supply and demand somewhat better synchronized, the VVT would consider the author's latest plays as he turned them out at his own pace.

Contrary to some published accounts, Ghelderode did not in fact collaborate or even participate in the staging of his plays. Unlike such other recent partnerships as those of Jean Giraudoux with Louis Jouvet, or of Jean Anouilh with Roland Piétri and others, Ghelderode's six-year association with the VVT was characterized by a certain distance. Ghelderode had, after all, written the first few of his plays with no prospect of production; even now he had little or no idea as to how his work might be staged, and he continued to feel that such details were best left to "professionals." His job, he believed, was to write the plays. Notwithstanding, Ghelderode's association with the VVT stands recognized among the more memorable and fruitful artistic collaborations of the twentieth century. By the time the experiment had run its course, around 1932, Ghelderode was fully established as a dramatist and approaching the peak of his powers.

Formed from the nucleus of a wartime entertainment troupe, the VVT first came into its own around 1924 and was notable for the innovative nature of its traveling productions. No doubt somewhat ahead of its time, announcing a trend that would take root only later in France, the VVT was truly a "popular" theater in both commonly accepted senses of the term, addressed to the "multitudes" and decidedly left of center in its political orientation. It was also distinctly if not officially Roman Catholic in inspiration, as were a number of theater groups that sprang up in France around the same time. Indeed, given Belgium's dominant Catholic majority the VVT could not very well have been otherwise. Perhaps most important of all, the VVT was a distinctly *Flemish* organization, aimed at reviving and fostering ethnic Flemish tradition through the newly recognized and embellished Flemish idiom of the Dutch language.

Ghelderode surely cannot have missed the irony implicit in his new situation: as an author schooled entirely in French for cultural reasons, he was about to reach his widest audience through the medium of Dutch translations in which he would take no active part. Years later French audiences would have extreme difficulty with the Flemish ethnicity of his plays, giving rise to rumors that the texts had originally been written in Dutch. Indeed, it is the "double" or "split" character of Ghelderode's plays that delayed their wider dissemination until the author had in all likelihood exhausted his inner supply of material and that continues, even decades after his death, to impede his worldwide reception as a playwright.

By the time of his first association with the VVT, Ghelderode had already achieved some esteem among readers for his innovative version of the Faust legend and was beginning to apply many of the same approaches to the legend of Don Juan. Johan de Meester, brought in from his native Holland in 1924 to serve as VVT director, found in Ghelderode's unconventional approach to myth and potential spectacle a nearly ideal match for his own "daring" concepts of stagecraft. First on the agenda, de Meester told Ghelderode, was a play to be based on the life of Saint Francis of Assisi, to commemorate the seven hundredth anniversary of the saint's death. True to his own convictions, or biases, Ghelderode made it quite clear from the outset that his would be – indeed, could be – no traditional "devotional" play, and that he would agree to provide such a script only if assured of total creative freedom. Thus assured, he proceeded with *Images de la vie de Saint François d'Assise* (Images from the Life of Saint Francis), first performed early in 1927 to resounding popular and critical success.

Predictably, a number of pious reviewers objected to the spectacle of Francis dancing on the stage amid a music hall setting in one of the scenes, but even they had to agree that Ghelderode's play, far from denigrating Saint Francis or his life, was generally affirmative in its approach and message. With the first collaborative venture thus completed to the satisfaction of both parties, Ghelderode went on to complete his *Don Juan*, also turning out during 1927 two shorter plays, *Escurial* and *Christophe Colomb*, that remain among his best-known accomplishments.

Fruitful though it may have been, Ghelderode's association with the VVT was somewhat less than tranquil, with frequent ruptures and recriminations on both sides. The first major quarrel erupted late in 1927 and lasted well into 1928. Ghelderode, for his part, felt that the VVT had reneged on a promise to stage *Christophe Colomb* and certain other efforts; the VVT in turn wanted from Ghelderode a different Faust play from the one he had already written. Ghelderode, meanwhile, would denounce the VVT as a captive of the Roman Catholic Church, hence obliged to compromise its artistic mission for its spiritual one. By 1928, however, neither Ghelderode nor the VVT could really flourish without the other. A reconciliation of sorts took place during October of that year when Ghelderode agreed once more to tackle a religious topic, subject as before to his conditions of total creative freedom. The result, *Barabbas*, turned out to be even more unorthodox than his treatment of Saint Francis. Notwithstanding, the collaboration was once again successful, and *Barabbas* remains among the most frequently performed and discussed of Ghelderode's plays.

The success of *Barabbas* was soon followed by that of *Pantagleize*, a political farce developed from a short story that Ghelderode had written as early as 1925. The play *Pantagleize* derives somewhat from the German expressionism then in vogue but also looks forward to the Theater of the Absurd that Martin Esslin would describe some 30 years later. Renaat Verheyen, the gifted young actor who had brought life to Ghelderode's Saint Francis, appeared once again in the lead and title role, delivering a strong and well-recalled performance. Taken together, the productions of *Barabbas* and *Pantagleize* represented the culmination of Ghelderode's association with the VVT. Not long thereafter it became clear that things could never again be the same.

During the spring of 1930, within months after the successful introduction of *Pantagleize*, the VVT was torn apart by internal dissensions that had nothing to do with Ghelderode. The Belgian actors' union, presumably responding to complaints from within the VVT, demanded that the VVT comply with a rather exhaustive set of new rules, dealing mainly with working conditions. There would, for example, be no more rehearsals after performances or aboard trains in transit from one performance site to another. Amid the general discord and confusion Verheyen and several fellow dissidents split off from the VVT to form a new company of their own, to be known as the NVT, or New Popular Theater. Ghelderode, inspired though he may have been by Verheyen's interpretation of his characters, was reluctant to support the new venture with any new plays, remaining at least nominally loyal to the original VVT.

Ghelderode's reluctance would come back to haunt him very shortly thereafter, following Verheyen's sudden death in October 1930 at the unripe age of 26. In some accounts of Ghelderode's life and career, it is implied that Verheyen's death caused the playwright to sever all connections with the VVT, or at the very least to stop writing plays for a while. In retrospect, however, neither allegation appears to be true, although there is little doubt that Verheyen's life and death did inspire one of Ghelderode's more innovative and memorable plays, notable also for what it reveals about the author and his approach to drama. *Sortie de l'acteur* (The Actor's Exit) was supposedly written in Verheyen's memory immediately following his death; Roland Beyen's research indicates, however, that the play was not actually written until three or four years later.[8]

Still rent by dissension, the VVT would survive, more or less, through the 1931-32 season, as would Ghelderode's association with it. No notable productions, however, would emerge from this final phase. Ghelderode himself, recalling the labor-management problems of 1930, saw them less as a cause than as a symptom of the VVT's slow dissolution. Such problems, he suggested, would have been unthinkable just two years earlier, when all concerned still burned with a "sacred fire" of enthusiasm. His conclusion, by turns bitter and wistful, was that such noble experiments as the VVT are by definition short-lived, as perhaps they should be. If such ventures do not self-destruct, as did the VVT, they might well lose the spark of innovation and lapse into the conventions against which they originally rebelled (see Beyen 1971, 244).

By the time the VVT folded, Ghelderode arguably might have been expected to succeed on his own. The experience had, after all, refined both his talents and his sense of the stage. What is more, the playwright was then at the peak of his powers, as the plays written in his mid-thirties would eventually prove. Unfortunately, the dichotomy between his Flemish consciousness and his French expression would continue to impede reception of his efforts, and without the VVT there was no ready performance outlet for his texts. Ghelderode's truly superior efforts of the 1930s – including *Sortie de l'acteur, Hop, Signor!* and *Magie rouge (Red Magic)* – would not be "discovered" until years later, by which time the author might well have been past caring. On the threshold of further discovery and promise, Michel de Ghelderode – his name change legalized by Royal decree in 1930 – instead passed through a period of obscurity, frustration, and eventual disgrace from which neither he nor his career ever fully recovered.

Disappointment, Disgrace, and Destitution

Faced with the marginal prospect of seeing his plays produced, Ghelderode during the 1930s seriously considered changing over to the short fiction that had brought him his first favorable notices. Notwithstanding, he continued to write plays out of sheer momentum until he apparently exhausted his inspiration. From his mid-thirties onward, Ghelderode also became increasingly reclusive, partly because of his declining health. Whether from his early bout with typhus or from the wartime shortages that had obtained during his convalescence, the adult Ghelderode had never been truly healthy – even as, well into his thirties, he appeared generally robust, even portly. Often accused of a hypochondria that he never totally denied, the author habitually complained of minor ailments even when his health seemed good. Around 1934 he drastically curtailed not only his alcohol consumption but also the convivial entertaining that had gone with it. Toward the end of 1936 his health suffered a sudden, precipitous decline that he blamed on cardiac asthma.

According to Beyen (1971, 285-92) and Blancart-Cassou (25-27), Ghelderode's increasing infirmity, while neither feigned nor imagined, might well have been psychosomatic, closely related in his mind to the perceived decline in his creative powers. In any case, as he approached 40 Ghelderode feared that he was losing his touch, perhaps his imagination as well, and saw fit to blame many, if not all, of his problems on poor health. The visible evidence was surely at hand: between Ghelderode's "crisis" in late 1936 and the end of

1942 his weight had decreased by half, from more than 200 pounds to little more than 100, with no conscious effort on his part. It is perhaps ironic that the best-known photographs of Ghelderode portray a cadaverous semi-invalid when the plays that they illustrate were in fact written by his robust, even jovial-looking former self.

Toward the end of the 1930s Ghelderode began serious work on the short fiction to be collected under the title *Sortilèges* (Spells) and published during 1941. Fantastic, even Gothic, in tone and inspiration, the tales in *Sortilèges* may well, in the view of Beyen, have been influenced by the mind-altering drugs, particularly morphine, with which the author was then treating his various ailments (Beyen 1971, 289). At the same time the writing of the stories may well have struck Ghelderode as yet another form of treatment; as early as 1919, alluding to his frail health, the author would indicate that his compulsion to write was all that kept him alive. Two decades later, at the outset of another world war, Ghelderode was desperately ill, presumably no longer able to write the plays that had established his reputation. The stories of *Sortilèges*, although below the standard set by Ghelderode's plays, emerge nonetheless as genre fiction of high quality.

With the outbreak of war Ghelderode's career entered what would turn out to be its darkest period. Increasingly unsure of his talents, seriously ill and quite possibly under the influence of morphine, Ghelderode would soon accept an offer that, unlike the VVT's, was fraught with potential dangers, professional and political as well as personal. To be fair, Ghelderode might well have thought himself "above" politics, given his reputation as a writer; on the other hand, a man of his demonstrated intelligence might equally well have anticipated some of the problems that might conceivably befall him.

Flattered, no doubt, by the recent revival on Radio-Brussels of certain earlier Ghelderode texts, some adapted from the "puppet" plays and others expressly prepared for broadcast performance, Ghelderode agreed during 1941 to appear regularly before its microphones, reading aloud a column to be written by himself, entitled "Choses et gens de chez nous" (Things and People from Home). Unfortunately for Ghelderode, as for Belgium and the free world at large, the airwaves of Radio-Brussels had long since been commandeered by the Nazi occupation. Increasingly ill and infirm, suffering once again from wartime shortages and cutbacks, Ghelderode may well have assumed that he had not much longer to live. In any case, what he then chose to see as a short-term solution to his problems would in the long run work strongly against him: Early in 1945, several months short of VE-day but with Allied victory all but complete, Ghelderode was summarily relieved of his functions at the Schaarbeek communal office, after more than two decades of service, for having "collaborated" with the Nazis by lending his presence – and his material – to Radio-Brussels during the occupation (see Beyen 1971, 293-302).

Arguably, Ghelderode's involvement with the Nazi New Order had been passive in the extreme. Unlike certain French intellectuals such as Robert Brasillach (1909-45) or Pierre Drieu La Rochelle (1893-1945), executed for their well-publicized – and published – expressions of sympathy with the New Order, Ghelderode had been no propagandist; his broadcasts were quite resolutely apolitical. Postwar patriotic sentiment, however, soon rose to fever pitch, and Ghelderode was in effect being censured for not *refusing* to work with Radio-Brussels in any capacity whatsoever. (Those who knew him, meanwhile, and those who had read his plays carefully, cannot have helped but notice the author's ill-concealed racial and ethnic prejudices.) According to Beyen, it is also likely that Ghelderode was at last being required to pay the full price for long years of strained relations with his colleagues at the Commune office (Beyen 1971, 298-301). During the war, moreover, Ghelderode had so frequently taken sick leave from his duties that his colleagues might have grown unaccustomed to seeing him around. In any case, Ghelderode would appeal his dismissal with much official correspondence, supported by character references. He had, however, grown truly too infirm to work, and before long he was applying not for reinstatement but for a retirement pension instead.

For years Ghelderode had felt neglected as an artist, denied the measure of recognition that he justly believed his due. Indeed, suggests Beyen, Ghelderode might well have assumed, desperately and no doubt absurdly, that the occupant Germans were more appreciative of his talents than the prewar Belgian government had been (Beyen 1971, 302-304). With Hitler's defeat he felt not only neglected but also persecuted, presumably for having been an "apolitical" artist. More than once the ailing, impoverished playwright would contemplate murder-suicide, involving his wife and their dog. As with the ill-fated Mariette, gas would be the chosen medium (Blancart-Cassou, 26).

During the spring and summer of 1946 the Ghelderodes – and their dog – revisited their former vacation haunts on the Belgian coast for the first time since the war broke out. Ghelderode, his disposition somewhat improved by the salt air and pleasant vistas, followed the progress of his case with interest, but with some measure of detachment. In May 1946 he was duly awarded back pay and pension benefits, only to be informed within one week that no funds were available to pay him. Finally, during October of that year the money began to trickle forth; Ghelderode, meanwhile, had gone without work or pay for the better part of two years. For the rest of Ghelderode's life his compensation would remain barely adequate to support himself and Jeanne; more than once he would fail to receive appointments or cash prizes that he had vigorously sought on the merits of his published work. His health, meanwhile, continued to decline, along with his perception of his talents. Although he maintained a number of works-in-progress – memoirs, short fiction, even the start of a novel – none would come to fruition. Only once more, with *Marie la misérable* in the early 1950s, would he attempt to write a play, and then in response to a commission. Ironically, it was not until after his retirement from active life, as well as from his job, that Ghelderode would receive the recognition that he had long craved and, in fact, deserved; even then, he might well have perceived the sudden flurry of attention as too little too late.

The Scandal of Success

No later than the fall of 1946, around the time that his pension was restored, Ghelderode began receiving inquiries about his plays from the French actress and animator Catherine Toth, who with her husband, André Reybaz, had recently founded the Compagnie du Myrmidon, one of the more noteworthy avant-garde theatrical ventures to surface in Paris after the Liberation. Ghelderode, no doubt cautious, even mistrustful, saw fit to ignore Toth's first few letters, but the lady was persistent, flattering Ghelderode with the assurance that his work was richly deserving of a wider audience. During the summer of 1947, with Ghelderode's permission, the Myrmidon performed two of his plays, *Hop, Signor!* and *Le Ménage de Caroline* (Caroline's Household), before an audience of attentive but generally puzzled critics. Soon, however, Ghelderode's name was in circulation throughout Paris, together with a growing reputation for innovative, unorthodox talent.

Late in 1948 *Escurial* was mounted by yet another director, René Dupuy, to considerable critical acclaim. It was not, however, until the summer of 1949 that *"la ghelderodite aigüe"* ("Acute Ghelderoditis"), in the memorable phrase of a now-forgotten journalist (Guy Dornand), was finally diagnosed on the Parisian stage. Before the "affliction" ran its course it would have reached epidemic proportions. Unfortunately, the sudden celebrity that now came to Ghelderode struck him as more perplexing than rewarding, hardly compensating him for what he perceived as nearly a lifetime of neglect and even persecution.

The French have always taken their theater seriously, with many competitions for the encouragement and training of young thespians. It was in such a context that Acute Ghelderoditis was first observed, when two of the nine companies vying for the third Grand Prix des Jeunes Compagnies chose works by Ghelderode as vehicles for their art. When those troupes finished first and third in the competition, the full spotlight of journalistic attention focused on a playwright of whom few readers had even heard and whose work proved most bizarre and shocking, even to the jaded Parisian audience.

Reybaz and Toth, attracted to the more outrageous among Ghelderode's plays, had chosen as their entry in the 1949 competition *Fastes d'enfer* (*Chronicles of Hell*). After they won first prize, Ghelderode's graphic evocation of venality and scatology, with evident undertones of blasphemy, gave rise to wild speculation among journalists as to the author's age, occupation, nationality, and beliefs. Jean-Louis Barrault, already assured of his place in French dramatic history although not yet turned 40, invited Toth and Reybaz to perform *Chronicles of Hell* at the Theatre Marigny, an offer they accepted. Reybaz and Toth did not, however, accept Barrault's subsequent suggestion, after two highly controversial performances in October 1949, that they cut the scandalous final scene of the play. The ensuing differences of opinion, aired both from the stage and in the press, reminded many observers and participants of an incident that they had read about in school – the "battle" surrounding the staging of Victor Hugo's Romantic drama *Hernani* in 1830. Indeed, Ghelderode – at the end of his powers and almost past caring – was about to become as notorious as had the young Hugo in the wake of *Hernani*.

Significantly, the Acute Ghelderoditis that now infected the French stage was confined mainly to the smaller "art" theaters and to the student groups from which the 1949 competition had originated. In those circles Ghelderode's immediate "competition" would come from three non-Frenchmen, notably younger than himself yet well past the first bloom of youth, for whom French was – even more than for Ghelderode – an acquired idiom. As Ghelderode's reputation developed, however belatedly, it would compete almost directly with those of the Russian-born Arthur Adamov (1908-70), the Irish expatriate Samuel Beckett (1906-89) and the half-Romanian Eugène Ionesco (born 1912). Ghelderode – his work formed under different influences and quite unknown to these slightly younger Theater of the Absurd practitioners – would nonetheless manage to hold his own in their company. Indeed, Acute Ghelderoditis would continue to "infect" the French stage until around 1953, when it would be routed by an even stronger infection destined to become chronic. Although perhaps intrigued by Ghelderode, the French, political by nature, would find even more seductive the reworked Marxism of Bertolt Brecht (1898-1956), Ghelderode's almost exact contemporary. Once Brecht and his Berliner Ensemble had taken Paris by storm in 1953, the Ghelderode moment would be over – although the vogue of Beckett and Ionesco would continue to survive for at least another decade. (Adamov, deliberately forsaking his initial Absurdist mode for social and political "relevance" in the Brechtian manner, found his career in decline and died a suicide in 1970.)

During the summer of 1951 a seriously ailing Ghelderode sat for the taping of the Ostend Interviews, subsequently broadcast in Belgium and later in France in 1951-52. In charge of the project was Roger Iglésis, whose production of Ghelderode's *Mademoiselle Jaire* (*Miss Jairus*) had taken third prize in the 1949 Paris competition. Jeanne de Ghelderode would later lament that Iglésis and his colleague, Alain Trutat, had taken advantage of her husband's infirmity and chronic fatigue, "leading" their "witness" and badgering him into positions that he might not otherwise have taken. Ghelderode's weakness might also account for some, if not all, of the distortions noted by Beyen as he compared Ghelderode's recollections with his own reestablished facts. Notwithstanding, the Interviews amply served their stated purpose, putting the hitherto obscure playwright in touch with his new, receptive audience.

A transcript of the Interviews would be published under the same title in 1956. Beyen, comparing the original typescripts with the published texts, noted considerable alterations and deletions, most in Ghelderode's hand and probably dating from 1954 (Beyen 1971, 41-45). Still, in the absence of a true Ghelderode autobiography and pending Beyen's publication of his study in 1971, the Interviews would long be considered authoritative, cited as such in most studies of Ghelderode and his work published during the 1960s.

During and after the period of Acute Ghelderoditis on the Paris stage, the author's belated fame and recognition continued to spread worldwide, with his plays being translated as far away as eastern Europe and North and South America. In the United States Ghelderode's growing reputation owed much to the pioneering work of David Grossvogel, who devoted a substantial chapter in *The Self-Conscious Stage in Modern French Drama* to Ghelderode's plays. Many theses and dissertations would soon follow, a number of them written (or at least begun) in Ghelderode's lifetime. Although somewhat bewildered by such sudden attention, Ghelderode spent as much time and effort as his health would allow in correspondence with his newfound expositors; several of his extant late letters, published by their recipients, helped to supplement a number of his cryptic comments in the published Interviews.

Still, the recognition Ghelderode long craved continued to elude him. Owing in part to his wartime involvement with Radio-Brussels, he was never elected to the Royal Academy of Letters in Belgium and was given short shrift the first time – around 1954 – that his name was mentioned in connection with the Nobel Prize for Literature. Unbeknownst to Ghelderode, his name would be proposed for that honor once more, just prior to his death, largely through the efforts of the Anglo-American drama critic Eric Bentley and a group of Bentley's American colleagues. After Ghelderode's death in April 1962, a member of the Nobel board conceded that, had the Belgian playwright lived until October, he would in all likelihood have received that year's literary prize, awarded instead to the American

novelist John Steinbeck (1902-68). It is doubtful, however, that even
the high distinction of the Nobel Prize could by then have sufficed to
raise Ghelderode's depressed spirits.

The Author's Exit and Its Aftermath

From his mid-fifties onward, Ghelderode had been obliged by his
worsening asthma to sleep in a chair instead of a bed. His legs,
meanwhile, became grotesquely swollen with an edema that
betrayed the deterioration of his cardiovascular system. Those rare
interviewers invited to visit the ailing playwright in his lair, a Schaarbeek apartment that he had shared with Jeanne and a succession of
dogs since the early 1930s, could not fail to notice and, in the event,
to photograph, the bizarre assemblage of memorabilia and playthings
with which Ghelderode had surrounded himself – tailor's dummies,
puppets, disembodied or beheaded mannequins, carousel horses
long since retired from service in carnivals – all doubly suggestive of
artifice and of death. Even in his weakened state, Ghelderode was
still playing a role, and the strange furnishings of his apartment soon
became part and parcel of the growing Ghelderode legend.

After he turned 60 Ghelderode became increasingly preoccupied
with the feverish dream of vision – "Not now, sixty-three" – that he
remembered from his youth. Was he, in fact, to die in his sixty-third
year, after his sixty-third birthday, or, indeed, in 1963? Jacqueline
Blancart-Cassou, who sees Ghelderode's obsession with mortality as
a major source of his creative talent, suggests that it may well have
been his *fear* of death that finally killed him, just two days short of
his sixty-fourth birthday. He could not have known, in any event, of
the Nobel Prize deliberations then in progress, and he might well
have greeted the news with indifference.

Unlike other artists and writers discovered only after death,
Ghelderode died in the *process* of discovery, with several major
studies of his work already in preparation. As those books and articles appeared throughout the 1960s, Ghelderode's reputation
continued to flourish and to spread, enhanced by new translations
and productions of his plays. Since 1965 samples of his work have at
last begun to be included in literary and dramatic anthologies. Some
of the earlier studies of Ghelderode's work appear less faithful to

their subject than to their own time, the 1960s, either forcing comparisons with Ionesco and Beckett or imposing "philosophical" discourse on Ghelderode's intrinsically instinctive art. Those same studies also tend to be hampered by excessive dependence on the Ostend Interviews, perpetuating factual errors about Ghelderode's life that would not be corrected until the publication of Beyen's critical biography in 1971. Still, the early studies remain useful for their insights into particular plays, and they served in their time to disseminate Ghelderode's works before a wider audience than had ever been reached before. Beyen's ongoing work, meanwhile, has helped to inspire a second generation of Ghelderode scholarship, with frequent international colloquia held to assess and appreciate the author's true contributions to world drama.

In France, the country that ushered Ghelderode onto the world stage and whose language he had appropriated as his own, the Acute Ghelderoditis of the early 1950s never reached a "chronic" stage, nor does it seem likely ever to do so. Although Ghelderode's plays remain in print at the Paris-based house of Gallimard, they are absent from the standard French repertory, no doubt owing to their abiding "estrangement" from the traditional French values of reason and logic. Elsewhere on the Continent, by contrast, some of Ghelderode's plays remain in the artistic repertory, as they do in Britain, the United States, and parts of Latin America. Ironically, Ghelderode's efforts appear to have survived him mainly in translation, their reception still impaired by the "language barrier" that has marked their fortunes since the 1920s.

Chapter Two

An Instinct toward Drama

Just as the mature Ghelderode tended to recall events the way they *might* have happened, but probably did not, so also did he distort the recalled chronology of his creative efforts, retroactively assigning dates to his plays and stories according to when he might have *liked* to write them. Such a practice, although surely an author's prerogative, tends to play havoc with the practice of literary history. Roland Beyen, in addressing himself to Ghelderode's work shortly after the playwright's death, had no intention of writing the authoritative biographical essay for which he has since become known. His original aim, considerably more modest, was to prepare a scholarly thesis tracing the possible sources of Ghelderode's plays. To do so, however, Beyen had first to establish a chronology of the plays. Almost as soon as he began doing this he encountered instance after instance in which the author had in effect "lied" about the dating of particular works. Thus alerted, Beyen began to delve deeper into the elusive truth, deferring publication of his literary-historical discoveries until *after* he had reestablished all of the pertinent facts in *Michel de Ghelderode, ou La Hantise du masque.*

In the series study *Ghelderode*, published in 1974, some three years after the biography and intended for the undergraduate as well as for the general reader-spectator, Beyen restores Ghelderode's plays to their true chronological order, allowing such subsequent critics and researchers as Jacqueline Blancart-Cassou to trace the author's authentic evolution both as person and as playwright. The Ghelderode who now appears before the curious eyes of reader-spectators is thus somewhat different, though no less talented or noteworthy, than the Ghelderode most visible during the years immediately preceding and following his death in 1962.

Ghelderode began to think of himself as a writer while he was still in his teens, and began writing in earnest not long thereafter. At the outset, he tended to vacillate between drama and short fiction and would later return to fiction (*Sortilèges*) when he felt that he was losing his touch as a dramatist. Notwithstanding, even Ghelderode's earliest plays display a confident talent that is lacking from even the best of his fiction. His first dramatic effort, written as if on a dare, shows a strong (if undeveloped and immature) sense of sight, sound and spectacle – precisely those elements that would assure Ghelderode's eventual reception on the world stage.

Written to "illustrate" a lecture on Edgar Allan Poe, presumably his favorite writer at the time, *La Mort regarde á la fenêtre* (Death Looks in at the Window) appears derivative not only of Poe, as might be expected, but also of the Belgian symbolist playwright Maurice Maeterlinck (1862-1949), perhaps best known for *L'Oiseau bleu* (1909; *The Bluebird*). Already in evidence, however, are a number of what would become Ghelderode's characteristic themes and procedures, supported by nearly all the potential resources of the stage.

Divided into six brief scenes, *La Mort regarde á la fenêtre* presents the final moments in the life of an aging Roman princess during the eighteenth century. The Princess's castle is dark and foreboding, an atmosphere intensified by harpsichord music followed by howling winds and ominous-sounding church bells. Besides the Princess the play's characters include a young witch and a sinister archdeacon. The table is set for a sumptuous dinner, held every year on the same date in November, but death has gradually reduced the annual guest list. Ultimately, the old Princess stands condemned to death for the neglect and denial of her late husband, César Chialevone, whose ghost materializes at the end to bring about the Princess's demise against a sonorous background of the wind and bells.

No doubt well suited in tone, theme, and atmosphere to complement a lecture on Poe, Ghelderode's initial dramatic effort also recalls, through the Princess's apparently merited death, the final scene of Molière's *Don Juan*, in which the protagonist is led to his grave by a ghost. Truly innovative, however, was the young author's skillful use of décor and sound effects to deepen the intended mood. At the same time *La Mort regarde á la fenêtre* clearly announces the major Ghelderodian themes of guilt, fear, frustrated love, and, of course, the hovering presence of death suggested in the play's title. Ghelderode would soon dismiss the play as juvenilia, however, considering it unworthy of consideration alongside his subsequent, mature work (see Blancart-Cassou, 55-57).

Shortly after the single production of *La Mort regarde à la fenêtre* at the end of April 1918, Ghelderode wrote a second short play that would, by contrast, be revised frequently and ultimately included among the author's collected works. Known in its final version of *Piet Bouteille*, the play was first known by the Flemish title *Oude Piet* (Old Piet) although written entirely in French. As in the earlier play, the presence of death hovers close as the 79-year-old Piet lies terminally ill, his impending demise eagerly anticipated by his wife and grown son. Three haglike town gossips are also on the scene, invited to "speak for" the speechless, dying peasant when the village priest demands his last confession. Only the town ragpicker, Jef, and Piet's blind granddaughter Madeleintje seem to mourn the old drunkard's imminent death. The three gossips, "confessing" in Piet's place, end up accusing him of causing young Madeleintje's blindness by kicking her mother in the abdomen during pregnancy. Only Jef seems ready or willing to refute the charge when the old man quietly dies. In a truly startling final scene Piet's accusers turn to face the accusatory stare of young Madeleintje who has suddenly, as if miraculously, regained the gift of sight and who has, moreover, witnessed the entire deathbed scene. The would-be denouncers thus stand denounced by their own actions, as by the implication that old Piet, far from being a criminal, might well have harbored saintly qualities.

A subsequent Ghelderode effort, *Le Repas des fauves* (Meal of the Savages), performed in 1919 yet neither published nor preserved, appears to have been a hastily conceived antiwar satire dealing with the conflict just ended. Ghelderode did not, indeed, turn his full attentions to playwriting until around 1923, when he began working for the Commune of Schaarbeek. *Les Vieillards* (The Old Folks), his next significant effort, was probably composed around that time, although Ghelderode later back-dated its composition to 1919, when the idea for the play presumably first occurred to him.

Much as it owes to the influence of Maeterlinck and others, *Les Vieillards* clearly announces Ghelderode's negative yet generally entertaining portrayal of human nature. Set in an asylum for the elderly, *Les Vieillards* presents a potential revolt among inmates reluctant to perform in an Easter pageant. Dressed in purple episcopal robes, presumably because the Apostles served as Christendom's first bishops, the 12 old men grumble about the task demanded of them, threatening to "tell off" the rich benefactor, himself dressed as Jesus, whose appointed role is to wash their collective feet. At times the old men's aimless questioning and complaining anticipates the dialogue of Samuel Beckett, particularly in *En Attendant Godot* (1953; *Waiting for Godot*). Here, however, the men's anguished grumbling will be both ended and discredited when they are "bought off" by the promise of a small gold coin to be handed to each at the end of the performance. Although well-conceived and well-plotted, *Les Vieillards* would remain unperformed for nearly 20 years until, retitled *Jeudi-saint* (Holy Thursday), it was aired as a devotional play by the Nazi-occupied Radio-Brussels on the appropriate religious holiday in 1942.

Jacqueline Blancart-Cassou considers *Les Vieillards* notable not only for its intrinsic merits but also because it is the last of Ghelderode's early efforts *not* to bear the imprint of his sustained experiments with puppetry and puppet theater, an interlude that followed not long thereafter. Around the time of his marriage in 1924, even as he mounted the hoax featuring the fictitious undertaker Philostène Costenoble, Ghelderode was deeply engaged in what may be seen as yet another hoax. This effort involved the preparation and eventual publication of marionette plays ostensibly "restored" from traditional spectacles performed in Brussels's Quartier des Marolles. To aid him in his efforts, Ghelderode actually acquired a puppet stage and set it up in his home. There is no evidence that Ghelderode ever performed puppet shows before an audience, or even for his wife; in all likelihood the *castelet* (puppet stage) served Ghelderode mainly as a laboratory for plotting his plays, which, although he claimed otherwise, sprang mainly from his increasingly fertile imagination.

Although the mature Ghelderode would, in the Interviews and elsewhere, credit the novelist Georges Eekhoud with "introducing" him to the puppet shows in the Quartier des Marolles, evidence strongly suggests that he had known and frequented the spectacles since childhood (see Blancart-Cassou, 61-62). In any event, his intense involvement with puppetry came several years after his closest acquaintance with Eekhoud and at a time when he was actively seeking – as with the poetry ascribed to "Costenoble" – a diversity of outlets for his prodigious creative energy. As in the case of Costenoble, the puppet shows allowed him to express certain budding talents and, at the same time, to deny authorship of work that he considered second rate.

Just as he claimed to have "discovered" the undertaker-poet, so also would Ghelderode claim to have discovered the puppet shows, subsequently transcribing and editing them with scholarly method to produce readable, playable scripts. On close examination, however, the texts have proved to be very much Ghelderode's own work, so marked by thematic concerns as well as by deliberate anachronisms, puns, and ironic touches aimed at a sophisticated, "modern" audience. They do, however, bear witness to considerable research and true scholarship on Ghelderode's part, showing him to be closely familiar not only with the entire Marolles repertoire but also with traditional marionette shows throughout the Low Countries (see Blancart-Cassou, 61-75).

Although consistent in spirit with their traditional models, Ghelderode's puppet plays continue to express the young author's growing satirical concern with priests, women, and marriage, as well as his preoccupation with the certainty of death. The medium of the puppet stage, which favors short, laconic speeches in the absence of facial expression, allowed Ghelderode to achieve economy of verbal style while developing the potential of physical action and visual interest implicit in his plots. Indeed, his apprenticeship with puppets, although lasting no more than two years, would change his dramatic technique altogether. Discussing the transitional effort *Le Cavalier bizarre* (*The Strange Rider*), Blancart-Cassou finds clear textual evidence of Ghelderode's puppet experience, causing her to agree with Beyen that the play could not have been written prior to 1924, despite Ghelderode's claim to have written *The Strange Rider* as early as 1920.

In many ways a reworking of *Les Vieillards*, *The Strange Rider* likewise deals with a group of old people awaiting death. Here, however, the number of elderly has been reduced from 12 to eight, including one woman, and the setting changed from an asylum to a hospital. There, one patient known as the Watcher (*le Guetteur*), stationed at the window, keeps his fellow patients informed of what is happening outside. Throughout the action the audience recognizes the strong possibility, neither proved nor disproved, that the Watcher has invented the entire scene in order to mock the others. At first only the Watcher can hear the sound of church bells, which he proceeds to mimic with his own voice; in time, however, real bells can be heard by characters and audience alike. The bells, it seems, are festooned on a huge, monstrous horse, whose "strange rider" can be none other than Death herself, come to collect one or more of the hospital's patients. Frenzied activity soon follows, punctuated by grotesque dances as the patients try to defy or to escape their fate. After confessing their sins in the imagined presence of Death, they hide under beds and bedclothes as the Watcher opens the door to admit their unbidden caller.

The monologue that follows, in which the Watcher addresses Death, is deliberately ambiguous, with the Watcher himself, according to Ghelderode's stage directions, unsure of whether or not he is playing a game.[1] In time the presence of Death appears to diminish, and the sound of bells can soon be heard, dwindling in the distance. Summoned by the Watcher, the frightened patients emerge from their hiding places, preparing to celebrate with drinks and more dancing the fact that they have apparently been spared. All is not over, however; even as the patients doubt the Watcher's reliability, the Watcher, still "watching," informs them that Death has indeed carried someone away – a newborn baby. Laughing to himself, the Watcher turns his face away as the old lady crosses herself, but accordion music is soon heard as the patients, in celebration, begin to dance "like puppets" (2: 25).

For Blancart-Cassou, *The Strange Rider* and the earlier *Les Vieillards* represent two panels of a diptych, one representing old people as they face the certainty of death and the other as they confront the emptiness of life (Blancart-Cassou, 72). In the later play, however, Ghelderode's approach to both plot and spectacle is stronger, more confident; through its rapid-fire dialogue and frequent, frenzied action it bears the unmistakable stamp of Ghelderode's apprenticeship with puppets.

As early as 1924 the aspiring playwright, with some help from the established drama critic Camille Poupeye, began to experience – and to experiment with – the various dramatic modes and currents that had surfaced on the Continent after World War I. The works that followed, described by Blancart-Cassou as belonging to Ghelder-

ode's "modernist" phase, were eclectic in the extreme, incorporat-
ing elements of Dada, surrealism, German expressionism and the
ground-breaking work of Luigi Pirandello (1867-1936). Although
Ghelderode in later years would dismiss any possible influence of
Pirandello on his work, claiming not to have heard of the Italian
master until his death, he in fact (as Roland Beyen would discover in
the course of his research) had written and published late in 1924 a
somewhat negative review of *Cosi è se vi pare* (1918; *Chacun sa
vérité; Right You Are If You Think You Are*). In Ghelderode's view,
Pirandello's play appealed only to the mind, leaving the rest of the
spectator's emotions untouched. For Beyen, Ghelderode's comments reveal his own intentions as a dramatist, foreshadowing an
accomplishment that in some ways would transcend Pirandello's in
that it would be more instinctive than cerebral (Beyen 1974, 18).

Like many fledgling playwrights before him (and no doubt some
to follow), Ghelderode proceeded to apply his recent esthetic experience to the reworking of traditional themes and subjects, starting
with Faust and Don Juan, in that order. His *La Mort du Docteur
Faust (The Death of Doctor Faust)*, published in 1926 with an introduction written and signed by Poupeye, was without doubt
Ghelderode's most daring and ambitious effort to date, as well as the
first to reach conventional length. Borrowing freely from expressionism and surrealism as well as from cinematic technique,
Ghelderode in *The Death of Doctor Faust* goes even further than
Pirandello in his exploration of "divided character" – *"le
dédoublement du personnage"* – and toward the truly theatrical
exploration of "reality" that would mark the best of his efforts from
the mid-1920s onward.

Set simultaneously in the sixteenth and twentieth centuries, *The
Death of Doctor Faust* uses the convention of *mise-en-abyme* (play
within the play) to question the traditional functions of legend and
spectacle. Aging, tired, consumed by self-doubt as well as by curios-
ity, the legendary Faust leaves his garret at Carnival time, against the
protestations of his assistant – here grotesquely called
Cretinus – only to find himself in the twentieth century, where a
third-rate drama based on the Faust legend is about to be performed
at the Four Seasons Tavern. Thereafter, the action is kept in motion
by the demonic presence of one Diamotoruscant, an agent of the
Devil if not the Devil himself. The action of the two plays at times

coincides, so indicated by parallel columns in published versions of the text. Besides the "real" Faust, Marguerite, and Diamotoruscant, there are "actors" cast in the roles of Faust, Marguerite, and the Devil, as well as "spectators" in the tavern who, predictably, have difficulty distinguishing one "spectacle" from the other.

Throughout *The Death of Doctor Faust* the artificiality of both "real" and "false" situations is highlighted by the use of such technological innovations as film titles, transparencies and electric sound equipment. Sound effects are abundant, including wind, thunder, and explosions, often accompanied by lightning and fireworks. The "real" Faust, meanwhile, attempts both to discover himself and to work out his destiny (even he, it seems, is familiar with the Faust legend) by seducing the 17-year-old Marguerite in a seedy hotel room. The scene in which Marguerite denounces Faust for refusing to marry her takes place before an audience of moviegoers both angered and saddened by the film they have just seen. Transferring their emotions to the scene now being played out in front of them, the moviegoers are about to intervene on Marguerite's behalf when Diamotoruscant, hastily closing his pact with Faust for the latter's soul, saves him from persecution by persuading the crowd that what they have just seen is publicity for the nightly Faust spectacle at the Four Seasons Tavern.

Organized into a prologue and "episodes" in place of conventional acts or scenes, *The Death of Doctor Faust* culminates in a final "episode" that shows the Four Seasons actors seeking refuge from the angry crowd. The "false" Faust, ironically, has gone into hiding in the "real" Faust's garret and is trying to persuade Cretinus of his identity as his fellow actors seek him from the street below. Marguerite, it seems, has committed suicide by jumping in front of a streetcar, and public suspicion has turned on the actors identified with the Faust legend. The actor-Devil, sensing a good exit cue, departs, leaving the actress-Marguerite to join the actor-Faust (and, in time, the "real" Faust) in Faust's quarters as an increasingly bewildered Cretinus looks on.

As the two Fausts confront each other in a truly post-Pirandellian paroxysm of mutual recrimination and denial, the other side of the stage fills up with a grotesque parade of judges, police, and other bizarre characters, their actions punctuated by sensational film titles describing Marguerite's fate. In time, the actor-Faust jumps from the window, giving himself up to the crowd, while the "real" Faust, egged on by Diamotoruscant, continues to look for his "double." In the end Faust, mistaking himself for his double (with Diamotoruscant's demonic help) shoots himself in the chest and soon dies, unsure of whether or not he ever *had* a soul. The lumpish Cretinus, meanwhile, prepares to take his master's place as he "consoles" the actress-Marguerite, now rendered senseless by what she has just witnessed.

In the Interviews Ghelderode would admit – perhaps truthfully – that he had no staging prospects in mind when he wrote *The Death of Doctor Faust* (EO, 79.) His intentions, he then claimed, were purely theoretical – to extend the scope of drama beyond the limits then conceived and practiced. Camille Poupeye, in his introduction to the published text, stressed the kinship of Ghelderode's play with the proto-surrealist efforts of Guillaume Apollinaire (Wilhelm Apollinaris de Kostrowitski, 1880-1918) and Jean Cocteau (1889-1963), both French poets who had ventured into experimental drama to test the limits of the medium. With *The Death of Doctor Faust* Ghelderode, although he had written some poetry (mainly as "Costenoble"), proved himself to be, indeed, a dramatist born and bred in ways that neither Cocteau nor Apollinaire could ever be.

Still, *The Death of Doctor Faust* is in many ways too "theoretical" a play ever to be fully practicable on the stage. Its initial performances, in Paris in 1928, were given in "closed" circumstances, before an invited audience of specialists. So too were those given several months later in Rome by the stage critic and theorist Anton Giulio Bragaglia. Although included from the start among Ghelderode's collected plays, *The Death of Doctor Faust* has seldom been performed since the 1920s. According to Beyen (1974, 22), it has been generally considered unperformable – unwieldy and expensive to mount, confusing to the potential spectator. The double influences of experimental and marionette theater then acting on Ghelderode contrived to produce an extremely "busy" play, overloaded with action and detail at the expense of coherence. For all of its flaws, however, the play soon proved indispensable to Ghelderode's developing career and reputation, since it was his publication of *The Death of Doctor Faust* that led directly to his association with the Vlaamsche Volkstoonneel (VVT), or Flemish Popular Theater, beginning late in 1926.

From 1926 until the early 1930s Ghelderode's career took a somewhat bifurcated path. On the left he produced scripts requested by his newfound "patrons," all the while reserving for himself a perhaps unexpected measure of artistic independence. In such spare time as he could muster, however, Ghelderode continued with his "own" work, most of which was, by prior agreement, offered to the VVT for first disposal. Among the plays Ghelderode wrote "for himself" during the period of his association with the VVT are the now-esteemed *Escurial* and *Christophe Colomb*, both undertaken in 1927. Before starting those plays, however, Ghelderode had first to finish work on his version of the Don Juan legend, from which he had borrowed time to prepare *Images de la vie de Saint François d'Assise* for the VVT.

Similar in concept and ambition to his version of the Faust legend, Ghelderode's *Don Juan*, subtitled "Les Amants chimériques" ("The Phantom Lovers"), remained unperformed until shortly after his death, although it had already been published among his collected plays. As late as 1959 Ghelderode had written to an actor friend that his *Don Juan* was perhaps too iconoclastic ever to be performed, yet at its first performance some three years later it was hailed for its "modernity" (Beyen 1974, 25). Like *The Death of Doctor Faust*, the play is nonetheless an experimental and derivative effort.

Ghelderode's Don Juan, like his Faust, is an impostor, in the event not an actor but a costumed Carnival partygoer. Ghelderode's dedication of the effort to the comedian Charlie Chaplin indicates his personal vision of the mild-mannered man behind the mask. Returning home from a costume party, the timid, anonymous would-be Don Juan heeds the blandishments of a *Bonimenteur* (Barker) and ventures into a dockside bordello portentously known as the Babylone. There he is greeted by the three "local goddesses" – Aurora, Diana, and Venuska – all overweight and over 50 years of age. Refusing the women's proffered favors, Don Juan is about to leave, backing out the door when he is quite literally bowled over by the arrival of one of the Babylone's regular patrons, a bluff, self-mocking black man known as Béni-Bouftout (roughly, "good glutton"), who urges him to stay.

In time the two men, close to argument, are joined by three more "regulars" – Théodore, Hanski, and Pamphile – respectively labeled by their attire and behavior as being blind, mute, and deaf. (Later in the action their handicaps will be revealed as disguises, as will the blackness of Béni-Bouftout.) Encouraged by the Barker, admired by Don Juan's presence and his choice of costume, the Chaplinesque intruder soon settles into the role assigned to him, eventually seeking an assignation with the truly unreal creature that looms behind the bar, identified as the Babylone's proprietress, Madame Olympia.

The Babylone, as envisioned by a Ghelderode still strongly influenced by expressionism, is a cross-roads of illusion and reality, a privileged location – perhaps less developed than the *maisons de passe* of Jean Genet or even the retreat to be imagined by Ghelderode himself for *La Farce des ténébreux*, wherein men seek to lose or possibly find themselves. Nothing is quite what it seems, and in time the pneumatic-looking creature behind the bar will stand revealed as nothing more or less than a wax effigy designed years earlier in order to "immortalize" Olympia's gorgeous former self. Observed by an ominous, ratlike figure identified only as *"le petit homme vert"* ("the little green man"), Don Juan proceeds toward his evident destiny, apparently followed during act 2 by the four "regulars" who, not to be outdone, don bizarre, archaic costumes of their own in pursuit of Don Juan's legendary prowess and of Madame Olympia's "ideal" beauty. At the start of the third and final act, the "form" of Beauty lies lifeless at Don Juan's feet, presumably savaged by the violent assault of Béni-Bouftout and his fellow regulars.

During the action that follows, the Barker (soon supplanted by Don Juan himself) mourns the death of Beauty; not long thereafter Don Juan prepares a symbolic murder-suicide. Sure that "Olympia" is dead at last, he is surprised to find himself still among the living, yet feigns death when the four regular patrons return unexpectedly. It is at this point that the black man reveals himself to be white, the blind man to be sighted, and the others without their affected disabilities. In the course of a stagy "funeral oration" for Don Juan and the object of his attentions, each man discloses the "reality" beneath his disguise. Théodore, for example, claims that he has chosen blindness after having looked too deeply into himself, and into other people. Pamphile has chosen deafness because he prefers his own conversation to noises from the outside world. To the mourners' amazement, Don Juan rises from the dead and is preparing to leave the Babylone with them when Olympia's voice calls out to him, beseechingly.

An elderly, skeletal hag draped in gauze, complaining of heart spasms, the real Olympia confesses the secret of her mannequin ruse, declaring her love for Don Juan and inviting him to join her in partnership, brandishing a well-filled purse. An equivocal embrace leaves Olympia dying, then dead, seeming no more human than the crumpled mannequin at her side. Almost as an afterthought Don Juan grabs the old woman's purse before fleeing the scene, only to find the little green man blocking his path, flourishing a wooden sword. Identifying himself as the "former" Don Juan, immediate predecessor, the grotesque, leprous-looking figure swathed in bandages further claims to have been Olympia's erstwhile lover and business partner, informing his apparent successor that the purse he has just stolen is filled not with cash but with unpaid bills. "Tomorrow you will be like me," he tells the horrified young man, removing the bandages from his face to reveal a missing nose and a woundlike mouth, the ravages of venereal disease. Don Juan flees in haste, the old man clinging to him and grappling with him as the curtain falls.

Some five years after its initial performance in Brussels in 1962, *Don Juan* was revived in France by the veteran performers Daniel Gélin and Micheline Presle to considerable critical acclaim. By 1967 the play's basic premise proved somewhat less shocking than might have been the case 40 years earlier. For Jean Decock, in a study published not long thereafter, the multiple illusions and disillusions, hoaxes and antihoaxes used by Ghelderode in *Don Juan* signals a final dismantling of myth, an ultimate denial of those heroic values still held dear by the Romantics: In lieu of love or even beauty, there remain only disease and death, with Don Juan's quest rendered quite as meaningless as Faust's thirst for knowledge.[2]

In any event, the traditional "moral" punishment for carnal knowledge is here replaced by the threat of disease, a quantitative standard instead of a qualitative one. For Beyen, however, Ghelderode's act of dismantling is less than complete because one "value" appears to emerge unquestioned – the value of *lying*. "In fact," argues Beyen, "even as it puts down the myth of love, this play exalts lying. Everyone lies in *Don Juan* because without lies there would be no love" (Beyen 1974, 75). The belated productions of

Don Juan proved that the play is, in fact, both playable and entertaining, considerably more so than *The Death of Doctor Faust*. As Beyen observes, however, the text that was published among Ghelderode's collected plays, on which those productions were based, was considerably revised from the original version prepared in 1926 and no doubt profited from Ghelderode's experience with the VVT (Beyen 1974, 25).

Chapter Three

Ghelderode's "Generous Adventure" with the Flemish Popular Theater

For approximately six years beginning in 1926, Ghelderode found a ready outlet for his talents as playwright-in-residence for the Flemish Popular Theater (VVT). In a speech delivered in 1956 although not published until after his death, Ghelderode would describe the mutual association as *"La Généreuse Aventure"* (the generous adventure), although it was fraught with disputes and the VVT itself eventually collapsed as the result of internal dissension. The arrangement was nonetheless flexible enough to allow Ghelderode's pursuit of his "own" work, including two short plays – *Christophe Colomb* (*Christopher Columbus*) and *Escurial* (both 1927) – that would in time attract a strong following among actors and directors and frequently be published in drama anthologies. Perhaps more significantly, two of the plays directly commissioned by the VVT, *Barabbas* (1928) and *Pantagleize* (1929), are now considered among Ghelderode's strongest and most memorable dramatic efforts.

Ghelderode's first commissioned text prepared for the VVT was *Images de la vie de Saint François d'Assise*, less a play than a succession of tableaux illustrating and, in Ghelderode's own way, celebrating the life of Saint Francis of Assisi. Still unpublished in the original French except for two excerpts printed during the 1920s, Ghelderode's version differs sharply from the stock "devotional play." Pacifism and even anticlericalism prevail, and the scene that proved most controversial among the contemporary audience showed the future Saint Francis dancing. Fortunately, the dramatic values of the VVT closely matched Ghelderode's own, and the young playwright was afforded considerable artistic freedom even in his commissioned occasional plays. Controversial or not, the play was

generally deemed a success, confirming Ghelderode's growing reputation as an avant-garde playwright of considerable promise.

Once the Saint Francis text was finished, Ghelderode resumed
work on his *Don Juan*, proceeding thereafter to explore legendary
possibilities in the life and career of Christopher Columbus.
Although the theme of the quest still looms large, as in his portrayals
of Faust and Don Juan, Ghelderode's *Christopher Columbus* is considerably lighter in tone than the two prior efforts, with a strong vein
of satire that presages the success of his *Pantagleize* (1929), written
expressly for the VVT.

Christopher Columbus

Still somewhat derivative of expressionism, Ghelderode's dramaturgy
in the short *Christopher Columbus* – a one-act play of three
scenes – borders on the playful even as it stops short of comedy,
anticipating in many respects the Theater of the Absurd that would
emerge in France a quarter-century later. Ghelderode's Columbus, as
portrayed in the opening scene, is already a "burnt-out case,"
blowing soap bubbles out of sheer boredom when he becomes
intrigued with their spherical shape, which reminds him of an earlier
suspicion that the world might be round. Visually entertaining, pep-
pered with ironic and potentially humorous anachronisms, *Christopher Columbus* allows Ghelderode to indulge his latent gift for
satire, as in a conversation between Columbus and the emperor
Montezuma on the virtues of civilization, in which they talk mainly
about whiskey and archaeologists.

The final scene has Columbus returning to America in the historical present – 1927 – just in time for the celebration of Charles
Lindbergh's transatlantic flight. Welcomed by *"l'homme-foule"* (the
crowd man), a single actor making crowd noises in the manner of a
one-man band, as well as by a gathering of dignitaries, Columbus is
quite as dispirited as he was before undertaking his voyage. Columbus welcomes Death, dressed as an admiral in full uniform, only to
end the play as a statue unveiled by Buffalo Bill Cody. "You have to
be a statue to understand," he observes, still morose as the curtain
falls.[1]

Although first produced (not, however, by the VVT) as early as 1929, *Christopher Columbus* remained relatively unknown and unperformed until the 1950s, when the prevailing theatrical climate proved especially receptive to its singular blend of irony, fantasy, and humor. Indeed, those critics writing immediately after Ghelderode's death tended to exaggerate the virtues of the play, ranking it high among his published efforts. By the 1970s, however, critical favor had turned instead toward *Escurial*, written later in 1927. On examination, *Escurial* proves to be a far more mature and dimensional creation than *Christopher Columbus*, showing rapid evolution in Ghelderode's talent, or at least in his self-confidence, during the first year of his association with the VVT.

Escurial

During the Interviews Ghelderode discusses *Escurial* at a length out of proportion to its relative brevity, implying that the play ranked high among his personal favorites, as well it should have. Inspired by two Spanish Renaissance paintings he had seen on a recent visit to the Louvre – one by Goya and the other by Velázquez – as well as by a strangely haunting phonograph record then in his possession, Ghelderode recalls being "followed" by the two men depicted in the respective paintings until they took form in his mind as the unnamed King of Spain and his red-haired jester, Flemish Folial. (The name Folial, derived from *fou* or *fol* ["fool"], would recur often in Ghelderode's later work, as would the enigmatic figure of the jester.) As the play took shape on paper, Ghelderode claims to have imagined, beyond the already rich setting of sight and sound, an olfactory background for *Escurial*, smelling of caves and mushrooms (see *EO*, 191-93). However much overtime Ghelderode's imagination may have worked in the preparation of *Escurial*, the result is truly remarkable, both as drama and as literature.

Set in the royal palace of the title, portrayed as musty and in disrepair, *Escurial* portrays the deathwatch for an unseen queen who lies mortally ill while the shabby, decrepit King, more inclined to self-pity than to mourning, mocks the Monk and jester, Folial, who attend him. The King has already forbidden the traditional ringing of the death knell and is unnerved by the howling of the palace dogs as they sense the imminent approach of death. Folial, defying the King's order to kill the dogs in order to silence them, manages instead to calm them, claiming to have a "way" with dogs as with kings. It is soon clear, however, that Folial is near the end of his powers; he is quite disinclined to entertain the King as bidden, pleading fatigue. The King, reluctant to be left alone, badgers Folial into what will be his final "performance," a paroxysm of role playing and soul searching that remains, in the minds of many critics, among the most remarkable, effective scenes in twentieth-century drama.

Inspired by a deep emotion that will soon express itself, the anguished Folial begins his jester's act by telling the King of a custom prevalent in his native Flanders. During Lent, he claims the townsfolk will choose a simpleton and dress him up as a king, wining, dining and saluting him, only to strip him of his raiment and honors once the merriment is over. As he speaks, Folial mimes the performance by stripping the King of his crown and scepter, losing himself in his act until he nearly strangles the King with his bare hands, toppling him from the throne. Gradually, the audience perceives that the conflict is quite genuine. The King, aware of danger, nonetheless responds with a loud, long laugh that causes Folial to release his grip and moves the action into a second stage by suggesting that the two men exchange costumes.

With Folial seated on the throne dressed as the King, the two now vent their contempt for each other, each using the disguise as "cover" for his true emotions. It soon becomes clear that Folial has long been the Queen's lover, spied on by the King, and that the Queen is in fact a murder victim, the King having poisoned her himself. When the Monk returns to fetch the King on the occasion of the Queen's death, he cannot tell them apart, and indeed each of the men claims to be King – Folial because he has enjoyed a queen's love. After a struggle, the King summons his executioner from the next room and orders that Folial be strangled, yet appears almost to regret his decision as soon as it is carried out. Wondering aloud to the Monk if jesters are eligible for absolution, he observes that they are harder to replace than queens. Dazedly, he then proceeds toward the dead Queen's chamber amid the multiple cacophony of bells, cannons, and howling dogs.

Even more than *Christopher Columbus*, *Escurial* would meet the perceived needs of French actors and directors during the postwar period, some two decades after it was written. Intensely verbal despite the prime importance of nonverbal elements, couched in highly expressive, even poetic French with great economy of means, *Escurial* was frequently performed in Paris after 1948 and subsequently all over the Western world in translation. Because of the play's brevity – approximately 25 minutes' playing time – a continuing challenge resides in the choice of texts to be performed before or after it on a double or multiple bill.

Despite the Pirandellian resonances implicit in Folial's dangerous, ultimately fatal game, it would be hard to prove in the case of *Escurial* a direct debt to the Italian master. Most of the themes and patterns to be discerned in the play have already occurred in Ghelderode's previous work; the question of identity, for example, underlies his presentation of both Faust and Don Juan, and the importance of sight and sound is already stressed in his first play. What is remarkable about *Escurial* is the way all the elements come together in a single, unified, spellbinding spectacle. Not until some five years later, after the collapse of the VVT, would Ghelderode again "bring things together" as in *Escurial*, and when he did so – in *Red Magic* and *Hop, Signor!*, for example – he would return to the Renaissance setting and characters so cleverly exploited here.

Although *Escurial* was first performed – outside the VVT – early in 1929, at first in Flemish translation and soon thereafter in the original French, Ghelderode's reputation during the late 1920s and early 1930s owed more to two full-length plays commissioned by the VVT, *Barabbas* and *Pantagleize*. While set respectively in biblical and modern times, hence without the resonant richness of the Renaissance background, both plays amply demonstrated Ghelderode's skill in writing longer plays and are among his best-remembered, most frequently revived efforts.

Barabbas

In the case of *Barabbas*, as with the life of Saint Francis, Ghelderode faced the challenge of treating religious subject matter without sacrificing, or compromising, his own resolutely anticlerical and apparently antireligious views. Having warned the VVT from the outset that they could not expect from him any conventional sort of religious drama, Ghelderode proceeded in *Barabbas* to approach the theme of Christ's Passion from the inside out, portraying a mute Messiah nearly eclipsed by the talkative, self-advertising characters surrounding him. In his study of Ghelderode Jean Decock subtitles his chapter on the play "L'Envers de la passion" (The Passion Turned inside Out; Decock, 75-100). Drawing on various legends and apocrypha as well as on the Gospels, Ghelderode portrays Barabbas as not only a criminal but also a political subversive – in short, a rabble-rouser. Barabbas is not, however, the only loud, talkative character in the play; also notable for their outspokenness are Caiaphas, Pilate, Judas Iscariot and Judas's shrewish wife, here known as Yochabeth.

Divided into three acts rich in spectacle and action, *Barabbas* begins with the title character locked up in an iron cage with the two thieves mentioned in Scripture, here portrayed as cowardly creatures toward whom Barabbas feels only scorn and disgust. Loud and abusive, Barabbas nevertheless carries the courage of his convictions, badgering his fellow prisoners to bear their crimes and condemnation with pride:

> Thieves, you make me feel sorry for you. If you go on whining, I will make a complaint about you and get the judges to grant me the favor of dying alone, without the absurd hangers-on that you are. Doesn't my presence fortify you? Aren't you proud to be executed with me? – when the most you deserved was a hurried execution on some accursed waste plot, before the gaze of mangy dogs. After all, how do you justify your title of condemned men, what's the inventory of your exploits? Can you honestly call yourselves murderers? I doubt it. Me, I am *a murderer*. My exploits? Seek them in epics and endless rhapsodic songs.[2]

In the absence of meaningful dialogue, the other prisoners being too cowed to argue with him, the arch-criminal proceeds to speak his case in an extended monologue that would suffice to tax the memory of many experienced actors. For Jean Decock (77), Barabbas's revolt is metaphysical as well as political, extending beyond the laws of man to challenge the laws of God and thus establishing Barabbas as a Promethean figure. At the very least, Ghelderode's Barabbas is a haunting, riveting character, well chosen to stand at the center of a parable portraying the human condition. Of particular interest is his character development, seen by some pious critics as a conversion, once he notices the inert figure of Jesus at the other end of the makeshift jail. Perceiving that the fourth condemned man is not a murderer but a victim, Barabbas will try to intervene on Jesus' behalf once he learns, from eavesdropping, that the man has been betrayed by Judas, whom he recognizes as a petty criminal from the underworld to which he himself belongs. With a touch of wit, however justified, Ghelderode portrays Judas, traditionally the treasurer among the disciples as a "fence" for stolen goods, hence a personage considerably below Barabbas on the criminals' social scale. "This Jesus was the leader of a band, like me, a rebel," says Barabbas. "His only mistake was to want to manage things with gentleness when violence was what was needed" (*SP*, 1:68).

During the second act, which begins with Yochabeth's angry recriminations against her husband, Judas, the other Apostles wander aimlessly about. Barabbas appears at first to have bargained for his freedom by becoming the stooge of the Roman officials and their priests, fawningly repeating whatever he is told to say. As elsewhere in Ghelderode's plays, however, the character is himself an actor playing a role; as soon as he is released, Barabbas reverts to type, becoming a rabble-rouser as before, his invective softened only slightly by his possibly mystical contact with the condemned Messiah. Wondering aloud what the priests have done and why, he says, "God, give me the gift of hating more still and of cursing better still. They have set me free and I can't understand why" (*SP*, 1:93). Gathering momentum from the sound of his own voice, he addresses a gathering crowd of beggars as follows:

> Comrades, a new age is beginning. It is the advent of the beggars.
>
> Everything has been overthrown. I am your king . . . not like the other that they are going to crucify . . . but a redoubtable king, with troops, weapons, a friend of the great, protected by the judges. It is paradise regained. We shall burn the Books of the Law. We shall break up the Ark of the Covenant. We shall sack the Temple. Everything is going to change. Crime will be legal. The wrongdoers will be the just. And I, Barabbas, am the one who will smash up the universe! (*SP*, 1:94)

The third act takes place in the shadow of Golgotha, the Place of the Skull, where Christ is about to be crucified. In the foreground a Showman and a Clown are pantomiming, for profit, the anticipated crucifixion when Barabbas appears. Delighted to see the real Barabbas, the Showman (*Le Barnum* in French, after the American circus

master), offers the rescued bandit a job playing himself in the new
show, which promises to enjoy a bright future. Iconoclastic as ever,
yet perhaps in his own way avenging the death of Jesus, Barabbas
physically attacks the Clown who would dare impersonate the Messiah and, refusing the Showman's offer in no uncertain terms, proceeds to tear apart the wooden stage on which the spectacle is
mounted. "And now I'll light up," he declares. "I like fire. I like
destruction. Let the fire consume the booth and spread to the city
and to Calvary. Let nothing but ruins be left" (*SP*, 1:111). In the final
scene, after a confrontation with Herod, Barabbas will repeat his
earlier rabble-rousing scene before the beggars, encouraging Jesus'
followers to join him in anti-establishment anarchy; he is fatally
stabbed in the back by the Clown, obviously one of the many
"enemies" loyal to Rome and to the establishment whose presence
he has suspected. Addressing Jesus with his last words, Barabbas
dies facing Calvary.

Doubtless unconventional in theme and approach, charged with
action both central and peripheral, *Barabbas* met with a mixed but
generally favorable reception from the VVT's usual public. The play's
ambiguities are such that those who choose to look for religious values in *Barabbas* can surely find them, while those more concerned
with the human, even historical values implicit in the Crucifixion and
in early Christianity will leave the play with plenty to think about.
Ghelderode's Barabbas is symbolically, irreducibly human, in revolt
against the human condition and its social manifestations, injustice
and inequality. A number of critics, understandably, have seen in
Barabbas the prototype of the existential hero, a precursor of Albert
Camus's Meursault as he prepares for the guillotine (see Decock,
77). Yet it may be argued that Barabbas, in purely Sartrean terms, has
chosen essence over existence in his adamant refusal to question or
change his behavior. In that respect, he more closely resembles Inès
Serrano in Sartre's *Huis Clos* (*No Exit*), who finds herself in Hell
because she has accepted without question society's condemnation
of her lesbian tendencies. Defined as an "outlaw" by the nature of
the law, Barabbas feels compelled to play that role to the hilt. In any
case, the questions raised by Barabbas's impassioned revolt remain
unanswered and unresolved at the end of the play. "Existential" or
not, Barabbas still emerges as a kind of hero.

Owing in large measure to his chosen posture, and powers of persuasion, as a rabble-rouser, Ghelderode's Barabbas demands some consideration as a potential "political" figure, champion of the downtrodden, bent on anarchy. At the time of the play's first productions, avowed "anarchists" still roamed the world, their views often confused (by outsiders) with those of orthodox Marxism. Barabbas, although he preaches "anarchy," might also be seen as an advocate of the revolution presaged and encouraged by Karl Marx and his followers. Barabbas's death is thus politically heroic, that of an advocate of the masses done in by the establishment. Arguably, however, the anarchy that he has been preaching is hardly an attractive or practical solution, so perhaps his death at the hands of the Clown is only fitting. It is noteworthy that the Clown stabs him in the back instead of confronting him face to face. The political question has thus been raised only to become blurred by perennial issues of human complexity. For Ghelderode, native and lifelong resident of a nominal monarchy trapped among major political powers, the "solution" of social ills proposed by politics seemed hardly more promising than that proposed by religion. Human nature remained pretty much the same, ultimately unaffected by professions or persuasion, either religious or political. The futility of politics, part of the background in Barabbas, would be moved to the foreground in Ghelderode's subsequent effort, *Pantagleize*, first performed by the VVT late in April 1930.

Pantagleize

Following the success of *Barabbas*, the animators of the VVT saw fit to take a chance on a play idea, proposed by Ghelderode, based on a fiction fragment he had written and published some four years earlier. The quixotic, even Chaplinesque, central character already had a name – Pantagleize – that was suitably enigmatic for the stage, suggesting, in its most accessible derivations, "all-earth," with emphasis placed, as in the case of Barabbas, on the character's humanity. All that remained was to surround Pantagleize with suitable action and supporting characters – a task for which Ghelderode, after *Barabbas*, was more than adequately prepared.

As Ghelderode would recall in the Interviews and elsewhere, the figure of Pantagleize was inspired by that of a lone man whom he once saw crossing a public square in Germany not long after the Armistice. As Germans, occupying forces, and leftist revolutionaries exchanged bursts of gunfire, the prototypical Pantagleize proceeded calmly on his way with his nose in a book, pausing only to glance at the darkening sky and unfurl his umbrella (*SP*, 1: 147). The man's total absorption in his private world, quite removed from the violence going on around him, fascinated Ghelderode at the time and would lead to his creation of a self-styled "professional philosopher," whose thinking has undermined his reason. Employed as a fashion journalist under a feminine pseudonym, Pantagleize has also ghostwritten, for pay, a well-known Marxist pamphlet from which he can quote lines verbatim. Notwithstanding, he has little interest in women's clothing, even less in politics, and would like nothing better than to be left alone with his increasingly inconsequential thoughts.

Set prophetically "in a city of Europe, on the morrow of one war and the eve of another" (*SP*, 1: 150), *Pantagleize*, whose style is somewhat derivative of German expressionism, ironically observes the "unity of time" so dear to the French neoclassicists: the action unfolds within a single day, between dawn and midnight. The day in question happens not only to be the International Workers' Holiday, 1 May or May Day, but also the fortieth birthday of the title character and protagonist. As the plot unfolds, the day will be charged with additional meaning by the prospect of a solar eclipse and by preparations for the revolution foretold by Karl Marx and his followers.

Awakened on his birthday by his black manservant Bam-Boulah (spelled Bamboola in Hauger's English translation) who works also as a bootblack, Pantagleize meditates aloud on his age, on his aimless existence, and on the "destiny" recently predicted for him by a fortuneteller. His deliberate platitude, *"Quelle belle journée!"* ("What a lovely day!"), sends Bam-Boulah into incongruous transports of joy that will in time be explained. Bam-Boulah, it seems, is one of the prime movers of the impending revolution, whose perpetrators regularly gather at the Objective Bar to discuss their plans in carefully encoded language. Unwittingly, Pantagleize has just uttered the password chosen in advance by Bam-Boulah and his co-conspirators as a trigger for the revolution. Bam-Boulah can hardly wait to share the good news with his comrades, and when Pantagleize, in time, just happens to show up at the Objective Bar, he will be greeted with a hero's welcome.

Combining traditional techniques with experimental ones, Ghelderode divides the action of *Pantagleize* into three acts subdivided not into scenes but into expressionist tableaux. Of particular interest in the tableau set at the Objective Bar is Ghelderode's presentation of Bam-Boulah's fellow conspirators, an exposition skillfully balanced between stereotype and individuation. In the original French, the characters bear allusive names, some of which George Hauger has attempted to imitate or paraphrase in English. In such cases Hauger's "equivalents" are given in parentheses. The ironically styled Innocenti, who tends bar at the Objective, is an embittered intellectual. Lekidam (Blank) is a limp-wristed young poet whose recited works sound like a parody of surrealism. Bergol (Banger), a bearded, crippled anarchist, bears the scars of many an earlier struggle. Also present, under light disguise, is the police detective, Posaune (Creep), who, like the conspirators, is drawn close to stereotype yet remains memorable as a character, thanks in part to his latent sense of irony.

The four revolutionaries (and Posaune) are already in place when Pantagleize wanders in, instantly identified by Bam-Boulah as the man of the hour. They then leave to proceed with their plans, whereupon Posaune grabs the telephone to report his latest intelligence to headquarters. His call is cut short by the sudden arrival of a fifth conspirator, Rachel Silberschatz, who knocks Posaune unconscious with a bar stool. The tableau then ends, with Rachel having made her first, enigmatic appearance.

As in the case of Bam-Boulah, Ghelderode's characterization of Rachel Silberschatz, however memorable, is unlikely to find favor with today's readers and spectators, for both Rachel and Bam-Boulah emerge as ethnic caricatures, the "Jewess" and the "Negro." Stereotypical from her long nose and thick glasses on down, Rachel is further typecast as the local *pasionaria*, exuding sexuality and leftist determinism in approximately equal portion, with the lines separating erotic love from love of mankind quite frequently and deliberately blurred.

The fourth tableau, opening act 2 and set in Rachel's rented room, is a masterful accomplishment on Ghelderode's part, marred only by the stereotypical presentation that, in all likelihood, betrayed the author's intolerance of cultural diversity. Climbing stairs in the dark, Rachel and Pantagleize are heard before they are seen, with Rachel berating her new "discovery" for his clumsiness. Once inside, Rachel's mood swings wildly between "command presence" and seduction as she tries to decide whether the "man of the hour" is a true visionary or, quite simply, a fool. As a woman of action as well as of passion, Rachel does not suffer fools gladly. Afloat on a wave of revolutionary zeal, for example, Rachel will tell the surprised and, no doubt, flattered Pantagleize that the two of them are about to become the Adam and Eve of the new Promised Land and invite his passionate embrace. Seconds later, when the telephone rings, she will tell him that her passion is aroused by the immediate need for action. Pantagleize, quite unprepared by his contemplative poses to follow the precipitous drifts in Rachel's rhetoric, soon allows himself to be assigned to the dangerous task of robbing the national treasury, a fund consisting of priceless diamonds stored in a suitcase. The predicted solar eclipse, meanwhile, serves as suspense-building background for Pantagleize's newly awakened interest in women and in love – a love confused, as in Rachel's behavior, between sexuality and brotherhood.

Once Pantagleize has left her room, Rachel places a call to her confederates at the Objective Bar and learns that she is being followed. Hearing a noise, she then fires her pistol and a brief struggle can be heard in the darkness, followed by the triumphant laugh of Posaune. Pantagleize, meanwhile, proceeds on his mission, emboldened by his need to please Rachel. When challenged by guards, he tells them to "go to the devil," an epithet that just happens to be the proper password of the day. Thus does he penetrate the inner sanctum of the bumbling, officious elderly General Macboum (Macboom in Hauger's version) and, mistaken for a diplomat of some kind, abscond successfully with the well-guarded suitcase. Still following Rachel's instructions, he then proceeds to the Objective Bar, where her fellow conspirators have already begun to divide the spoils of the revolution. Bam-Boulah, for example, proclaims himself president for no other reason than that he is a "good nigger" (*SP*, 1: 190). Innocenti, properly skeptical of Pantagleize and his omenlike pronouncement, informs his confederates that the revolution was not, indeed, planned for that day and suggests that dire consequences are to follow.

Divided in their opinions, the revolutionaries are bickering when Pantagleize appears, bearing the stolen satchel. In fact, Innocenti's suspicions are justified, and as the rebels gather fresh courage from Pantagleize, drinking to celebrate their victory, they are served by police officers disguised as waiters. Establishing his bona fide status by citing his recent encounter with Rachel, the unlikely oracle and prophet Pantagleize joins in the revels, soon mounting a table to deliver an inspirational "victory" speech that is almost as bizarre, in form and in content, as Lekidam's poetry.

Doubly intoxicated by spirits and by the sound of his own rhetoric, Pantagleize barely notices as his listeners are knocked unconscious, one by one, by the waiters standing behind them. He assumes that they have simply fallen asleep and tries to awaken them with even wilder flights of fancy. Posaune is also present at the gathering, disguised as a potted palm. When at last Pantagleize despairs of his audience, he addresses the palm tree, expressing little surprise when it speaks back but nonetheless knocking it to the ground for what it has said to him. Pantagleize then flees into the street as Posaune sends one man after him, asking the others to place the unconscious Innocenti, Lekidam, Bam-Boulah, and Bergol in the meat cooler to await further disposition.

Still clutching the suitcase, Pantagleize returns to the room of Rachel Silberschatz, regaling her with accounts of his exploits and declarations of his love, playing out the rhetorical impulse first unleashed atop a table back at the Objective Bar. Pacing back and forth in transports of eloquence, he perceives only when he kisses Rachel that he has been walking through spilled blood and that the young woman is quite dead, although sitting more or less upright in her chair. Embarrassed, suddenly at a loss for words, Pantagleize abruptly flees after telling the corpse of his hopes that they might meet again.

The third and final act of *Pantagleize* begins with the eighth tableau, in which Pantagleize, unwittingly reversing his next previous performance, speaks to a living person disguised as a corpse. The body is that of Posaune, apparently trying to improve on his earlier camouflage as a potted palm. By now, most of the town has been laid waste by aimed and stray gunshots. As Pantagleize speaks to the "dead man" of his recent experiences, General Macboum marches through with a detail of soldiers to survey the toll of death and destruction. No sooner have the military men marched out the way they came than Posaune comes suddenly "to life," rising to his feet and cagily engaging Pantagleize in conversation. As the police detective tries to separate the would-be revolutionary from his satchel, the two men proceed on their way through a hail of bullets. Finally, Posaune stuns Pantagleize with a blow to the back of the neck and leads him away as one would guide the steps of a drunk.

In the ninth tableau a "kangaroo court" has been set up for the trial and disposition of the captured revolutionaries. Six masked councilors, presided over by a generalissimo, will hear pro forma defense pleas provided by a figure known only as the *"avocat distingué"* ("distinguished counsel"). First to appear before the tribunal is General Macboum, charged with negligence in allowing the treasury to be stolen. Before long, however, he is honored for his long years of faithful service as commandant of the central depot for the issue of mess kits and is dismissed. The revolutionaries, by contrast, will each be sentenced to death and summarily executed after being allowed to speak his piece, with little more than a token "defense" on the part of the distinguished counsel.

Ironically, it is in this final scene, as the conspirators prepare to meet their death, or fate, that Ghelderode's characterizations are most skillfully realized. Lekidam babbles incoherently in what appears to be blank verse, the case-hardened Bergol limits his speech to harsh expletives, and Bam-Boulah suddenly turns coward, pleading a case of mistaken identity. "Boss, that not me," he tells the Generalissimo. "That other nigger. He also called Bamboola. I good Bamboola. He bad" (*SP*, 1: 212). Innocenti, by contrast, faces death with resignation and a kind of dignity. Admitting that he is a former university professor of law and social sciences and that "Innocenti" is indeed a pseudonym, the would-be waiter goes on to describe himself as a revolutionary of the old school, committed to the ideal of revolution even as he foresaw the failure of the attempt that has led to his arrest. True to his long-held convictions, he willingly anticipates sharing the fate of his co-conspirators, for whom he feels both love and scorn.

Offered the prospect of clemency, Innocenti perseveres in seeking his own execution, claiming that his hatred, accumulated during a lifetime of struggle toward revolution, renders him unfit for service in any "constructive" revolution that might be yet to come. In his final line, as he prepares to follow the others, he looks forward to the "operation" that will free him of his "disease" – perhaps his hatred, perhaps life itself. The tribunal then prepares to close, having dealt with the last of the accused, when Posaune suddenly arrives with Pantagleize in tow. Getting ready to leave, the judges are both impatient with Posaune's tardy arrival and somewhat unwilling to take the new "defendant" seriously.

As Posaune, the hard-working detective, proudly presents his carefully built case against Pantagleize, based mainly on his own observations, the Generalissimo remains incredulous, asking the defendant if he is in fact a revolutionary, to which Pantagleize replies that he is a fashion journalist, adding various platitudes about destiny, love, and the solar eclipse. The distinguished counsel then steps forward to dismiss and/or defend Pantagleize as a mere lunatic whose conviction might well result in a miscarriage of justice. The Generalissimo, meanwhile, suspects Pantagleize of faking madness in order to avoid prosecution. All is relative, suggests Pantagleize, when allowed to speak for himself. Perhaps he is both a real and a false lunatic, depending on how others perceive him. In any case, Pantagleize concludes, he has been a failure in life, having lost with Rachel's death his last chance at true love. The Generalissimo, unmoved, concludes that Pantagleize will be no great loss to society and dismisses the tribunal, leaving the defendant as bewildered as ever.

In the published text of *Pantagleize* the "real" play ends as the distinguished counsel, Posaune, and two armed guards leave the courtroom singing a soldiers' ditty that has been heard off and on throughout the action. In practice, however, *Pantagleize* is rarely performed without the "optional" final scene, in which what has been implied becomes explicit. The scene opens with the Generalissimo examining the bodies of Bam-Boulah, Lekidam, Bergol, and Innocenti in the presence of a junior officer who recalls that the would-be revolutionaries died "like puppets," with no defense and little visible reaction. Soon the voice of Pantagleize is heard from offstage, inquiring as to where he might find "the exit." Stumbling into view, his hands outstretched against the darkness of midnight, Pantagleize speaks of his imminent departure for an ideal country like the one to which he wanted to take Rachel. Discovering the bodies of the other revolutionaries, he may or may not perceive that they are dead as he speaks to them of the conflict just ended. Still seeking an exit, Pantagleize climbs a prison wall and is about to escape when the junior officer calls out to tell him that he has dropped his umbrella. As he returns to retrieve it, groping about in the dark, the officer summons the firing squad and gives the proper order. Pantagleize falls, mortally wounded, calling out a last message of love for Rachel, whose surname he cannot recall. The officer, noticing that Pantagleize is not yet dead, fires a coup de grâce into the back of the prisoner's neck. Pantagleize at last expires, after commenting once more on the "lovely day."

"Optional" or not, the scene depicting Pantagleize's death underscores the basic pessimism of the play bearing his name. If Bam-Boulah has died as a coward and Innocenti as kind of hero, the title character dies as he has lived, in a state of benign befuddlement that hardly qualifies him for a hero's role. Like the Bérenger of Eugène Ionesco's *Rhinocéros* (1960), who, at the end of the play, simply *cannot* conform no matter how hard he tries, Pantagleize is last glimpsed as the hapless victim of forces beyond his control. There are simply no affirmations in the world of *Pantagleize*, and no truly affirmative characters.

Still somewhat stylistically derivative of expressionism, Ghelderode's procedure in *Pantagleize* relates also to the "objective" techniques of Bertolt Brecht, whose dramaturgy is even more firmly rooted in Expressionist principles. As Jean Decock observes (67), Ghelderode in *Pantagleize* has happened, perhaps by accident, on the *Verfremdungseffekt* (alienation effect) later to be sought and explored in Brecht's theoretical writings yet seldom achieved in that dramatist's plays. In *Pantagleize* the spectator is alienated or at least distanced from the characters, including Pantagleize. Whatever Ghelderode's intentions, *Pantaglieze* is even more than *Barabbas* a most anti-Aristotelian "object lesson" in which the audience is actively discouraged from "identifying" with any of the situations or characters. Unlike Brecht, however, Ghelderode in *Pantagleize* has no political agenda. His agenda, if any, is quite resolutely apolitical, questioning the value of any and all efforts to change or to "improve" society. Arguably, *Pantagleize* is among the most negative plays of its time, anticipating in its deep-dyed pessimism the dark, dehumanized theatrical visions of Adamov and Ionesco. Perhaps not surprisingly, *Pantagleize* would often be revived during the heyday of the Theater of the Absurd, although less frequently in France than elsewhere.

Like *Barabbas*, *Pantagleize* was initially performed to mixed reviews; not long thereafter dissension erupted within the VVT, with Renaat Verheyen among the dissidents. By the end of 1930 Verheyen was dead, having failed in his attempts to elicit new Ghelderode texts for his own theater company. For all practical purposes, the "generous adventure" had come to an end, although what remained of the VVT would produce two more Ghelderode efforts, *Oceaanvlucht/Atlantique* (1930) and *De Sterrendief/Le Voleur d'étoiles* (The Star Thief, 1932), both badly received by critics.

By 1932, however, Ghelderode had long since resumed writing plays "for himself" during office hours, profiting from what he had learned about stagecraft during his years with the VVT. Increasingly, he turned both inward and backward for his inspiration although he would in fact write (in 1931) one more play in the derivative expressionist mode of *Don Juan* and *Pantagleize*: *Le Club des menteurs* (Liar's Club), which would later prove among the more popular of Ghelderode's lesser efforts, combining in one brief act the themes and concerns of *Don Juan* and, in a sense, of *Escurial*. Set in the historical present in a shabby café, *Le Club des menteurs*, true to its title, deftly exposes the lies and illusions that sustain both the fading hostess Luna and her band of customer-admirers, each of whom pretends to be something he is not. The past, however, soon proved a more forceful lure than the present. *Red Magic*, also written in 1931, had opened for Ghelderode the rich vein of theme and character from which he would mine some of his strongest and best-remembered plays.

Chapter Four

The Renaissance Revisited

Left to his own devices even as he remained nominally under contract to the declining VVT, Ghelderode returned in search of material to the time frame of his two previous "personal" efforts, *Christopher Columbus* and *Escurial*. Freed from any constraint of having to deliver a "message" the playwright's imagination actively sought, and readily found, in the late Middle Ages and early Renaissance a fertile source of archetypal characters and situations to represent the human "truths" – most of them negative or at least disquieting – that lie just beneath the surface of *Barabbas* and *Pantagleize*. Still young (in his early thirties), Ghelderode embarked on what appears to have been a near frenzy of creative activity. By the time his health began to fail in 1936-37, he would have turned out no fewer than five plays later recognized among his finest and most memorable – *Red Magic* (1931), *Lord Halewyn* (1934), *Miss Jairus* (1935), *Hop, Signor!* (1936), and *Chronicles of Hell* (1937), all set in the distant past, as was the remarkable "puppet" drama *Le Siège d'Ostende* (1933), regrettably not published until nearly 20 years after Ghelderode's death.

Also dating from this period but set in modern times is Ghelderode's impressive homage to Renaat Verheyen, *Sortie de l'acteur*, back-dated by the author to 1930 but actually composed, as Beyen has ascertained, between 1933 and 1935. Ironically, most of the plays dating from the 1930s would not be performed until at least 15 years later, by which time Ghelderode had, for all practical purposes, discontinued writing plays.

Red Magic

Among the first efforts normally assigned to the post-VVT period is *Red Magic*, written as early as 1931 but without the VVT in mind.

One of Ghelderode's few plays of the period to be first performed during the 1930s (in Brussels in 1934 and in Paris during 1938), *Red Magic* confirmed the author's reputation for unorthodox and memorable drama, attracting the attention of those French actors and directors who would subsequently "remember" Ghelderode in the years after World war II. For many critics and observers, *Red Magic* remains among the most typical and characteristic of Ghelderode's mature plays, both broadening and deepening the verbal and visual mastery present in *Escurial*.

Like the decrepit, half-mad monarch of *Escurial*, the main character of *Red Magic* is a late-medieval or early-Renaissance grotesque, in the present case an obese, obsessed miser known only as Hieronymus, the latin form of Jerome. In the course of a highly memorable opening scene consisting of a long soliloquy, Hieronymus takes inventory of his many possessions, including coins bearing both male and female likenesses. As he examines the coins he impulsively hatches a scheme to "breed" his "male" and "female" coins toward the procreation of innumerable shiny offspring. Hardly saner than the king of *Escurial*, Hieronymus, although not a ruler, is clearly a megalomaniac, seeking absolute power through absolute wealth. His ambition is to own the world, or at least all of the world that he knows, in order to maintain total control of his surroundings. Unlike other misers in literature as in life, Hieronymus has never, until now, sought to increase his wealth, preferring instead to savor its measure in an oft-repeated ritual of inventory. Indeed, what strikes him as most appealing about the "breeding" of his coins is that it offers him the prospect of return without investment.

Among his possessions Hieronymus counts also his wife and her clothes, a guard dog that saves money on food by eating its leash, and a ghost who presumably came with the house and helps to frighten off intruders. In time the spectator learns also that Hieronymus's wife, Sybilla, is still a virgin, Hieronymus having withheld himself from her as he has withheld his money from banks and bankers. In place of the child that Sybilla presumably wants, Hieronymus has given her a baby doll that, after all, costs nothing to feed. Last but by no means least, yet almost as an afterthought, Hieronymus counts among his possessions his immortal soul, which he has deliberately kept pure of the seven deadly sins, especially lust. Regarding the sin of avarice, Hieronymus prefers to describe himself as thrifty

(*"économe"*). After all, he wonders aloud, who has ever seen a fat
miser?

Oddly, Hieronymus has managed to grow fat without eating, as
has the obnoxious monk who pays a daily call to remind Hieronymus
of his mortality. When Sybilla rises from a sleepless night, interrupt-
ing her husband's inventory to tell him that she is hungry, he
encourages her to feast with her eyes on the food depicted in his art
collection, adding that he does not like fat women. Soon the Monk
happens by on his morning rounds, and the two men trade insults
regarding their shared, if unexplained, corpulence. Arguably, the
Monk is Hieronymus's double as well as his antagonist, helping to
bring about the miser's downfall.

Once he has crossed the threshold of reason by deciding to
"breed" his money, Hieronymus easily falls prey to a scheme suggested to him by the local beggar, Romulus. Romulus, it seems, has a
friend named Armador, an alchemist currently fleeing persecution
for having transformed baser metals into gold. Again enchanted by
the prospect of profit with little or no investment, Hieronymus
agrees to shelter Armador under his roof, offering not only his basement as a laboratory but also his wife, as the virgin whose blood will
be needed for Armador's experiments (hence the "Red Magic" of the
play's title.)

By now, of course, the spectator has begun to suspect that
Sybilla and Armador are already lovers, or would like to be, and that
Romulus's outrageous suggestion is nothing more or less than a plot
to bring the pair together under Hieronymus's roof and nose.
Hieronymus, however, is so blinded by greed and the lust for power
that he readily agrees, announcing, in a shorter soliloquy, his intention to "mend his ways" – in this case switching from virtue to
vice – once he is assured of the absolute power that Armador's
experiments promise to bring him: "What is happening to me? If it's a
dream, it's stupendous, and I'm a dream better off. If it's real . . .
then I shall be liberal, I shall live like a gentleman. I shall visit courte-
sans. The good time will have come, the end of hardship, fasting, cal-
culation" (*SP*, 2: 13).

At the start of act 2 a full day has passed, and Hieronymus, his
ear to the floor, anxiously awaits news of what is going on down-
stairs. In an extended soliloquy interrupted but not curtailed by
dialogue with Romulus and with the Monk, Hieronymus begins to

suspect, correctly, that he has been duped, even robbed, and threatens to kill Armador. Increasingly inflamed by imagination and resentment feeding off each other, Hieronymus ends by acting out the murder of Armador just as Armador himself arrives from the basement laboratory. Stagily outraged by the scene of his own death, Armador berates Hieronymus for his ingratitude. After all, he claims, his experiments have just made Hieronymus incredibly rich. Fawning, groveling, vainly trying to "eat" his words, Hieronymus curries favor with the alchemist, nearly bursting with delight when Armador hands over a sample of his "product," in fact a coin taken from Hieronymus's own coffers. Hieronymus is about to accuse Armador of counterfeiting when the latter sends him out to buy some wine, claiming that it is needed in the alchemical process.

During Hieronymus's brief absence, Armador is examining the miser's hoard when Sybilla appears, disheveled and clearly transformed by her night of love with Armador. Their conversation soon reveals that they are former childhood sweethearts. Reunited with Sybilla, Armador now proposes that they flee abroad with Hieronymus's stolen funds, operating a tavern and brothel in a port town until they are rich enough to retire to the countryside. Their conversation is soon cut short by the return of Hieronymus, now burdened with six flasks of wine. Armador quickly leaves, warning Sybilla to remain silent while he is out of the room. Faced with her husband's hated presence, Sybilla does even more than she has been told to do, credibly imitating a statue, or perhaps a member of the living dead. Hieronymus, increasingly outraged by Sybilla's refusal to answer his questions about Armador's experiments, denounces and strikes his wife, threatening to disrobe her in search of gold stains when Armador returns, bearing what appears – and sounds – to be a sack full of coins.

Breaking his long habit of abstinence, Hieronymus invites Armador to share the wine that he has just bought with the "sample" coin. Armador, feigning drunkenness, claims that he carries the alchemical formula on his person, together with a mystical black gem that confers and assures immortality. When Armador further feigns loss of consciousness, Hieronymus, increasingly intoxicated, predictably strips Armador of both document and jewel. When the Monk unexpectedly drops by, Hieronymus invites him to join in the celebration of a recent inheritance and announces his intention to leave

all of his earthly possessions to the Church. After all, Hieronymus
reasons, he has just obtained the gift of immortality, and the Church
will have an eternity to wait. Unknown to Hieronymus, the Monk has
been part of the scheme against him all along and can hardly wait for
Hieronymus to succumb to his unaccustomed intake of wine.

Once Hieronymus has passed out, more or less on schedule, the
Monk calls out to his three co-conspirators for help in heaving the
miser's bulk atop the hoard inside his treasure chest, but only after
they have substituted counterfeit coins for the real ones. Armador
and Sybilla depart for another night of love before leaving town at
dawn; the Monk departs too, leaving only the beggar Romulus to
keep watch over the sleeping Hieronymus. Soon thereafter, the miser
rouses briefly, raising the lid of his coffer as he revels in the tactile
presence of his "gold" beneath him. As the curtain falls on act 2,
Romulus laughs uproariously but silently, his presence unnoticed
and unsuspected by the drunken miser as he recloses the lid of his
trunk from inside.

At the start of the third and final act Hieronymus awakens and
raises the lid of his coffer, indulging in another lengthy monologue
as he prepares to reap the double benefits of immortality and absolute wealth. Hearing Sybilla's amorous shrieks and moans from
below, he promises to begin his new "life" with a visit to prostitutes.
Although he has told Sybilla that he detests obesity in women, he
now vows to seek the fattest women he can find, the most "meat" for
his money. Mistaking Romulus for the household haunt, Hieronymus
exits quickly, whereupon Romulus summons his co-conspirators to
discuss changes in their plan. Hieronymus's unexpected departure
might well foil their scheme to have him arrested at dawn on charges
of counterfeiting, after which they will divide the real gold into four
equal portions and make good their escape. There is, however, no
honor among thieves, and the Monk warns the lovers that Romulus is
about to betray them in order to collect more than his share of the
booty. Armador fatally stabs Romulus and hides his corpse in the coffer as the now-lascivious Monk follows Sybilla upstairs for an assignation tacitly approved by Armador.

Howling in anguish, fearing contagion and pursued by
"enemies" both real and imagined, Hieronymus returns early from
his "night of love." The experience has quickly turned disastrous,
and he is now fleeing an angry brothelkeeper whom he paid with a

coin instantly recognized as counterfeit. The Monk stumbles down from above, either drunk or (possibly) poisoned, just as the pimp and the law officers arrive all at once. Armador and Sybilla, disguising their voices as well as their faces, manage to slip down the back stairs before the officers find Romulus's body atop the counterfeit coins, charging Hieronymus with both crimes. (In a fit of pique, Hieronymus has stabbed the doll-child with a knife; the doll's presence at the scene suggests collusion with "dark forces," strengthening suspicion of his guilt.) As he is led away to certain condemnation and death, Hieronymus remains oddly detached from the experience, honestly believing himself to be immortal.

Inevitably compared to such legendary literary misers as Molière's Harpagon and Balzac's Grandet, Hieronymus nevertheless remains closer to symbol than to stereotype or archetype. Visibly and audibly approaching madness even as the play begins, never fully credible as can be discerned from his outrageous speeches, Hieronymus is memorable mainly for his almost palpable fear of the human condition, including both life and death. He is man in flight from himself, seeking in absolute power a refuge from the ravages wrought by the "seven deadly sins." Thus does Ghelderode, carefully avoiding the political "relevance" demanded by the VVT, manage still to question the maintenance of wealth for its own sake. As in his earliest effort, written in homage to Poe, Death still looks in at the window and takes what she (or he) can find. To be sure, Hieronymus, as he claims, is quite innocent of the charges leveled against him; still, it is hard to mourn his impending death. Having denied life in hopes of saving his own, he stands condemned in the eyes of both playwright and spectator as a member of the "living dead," outshone despite his eloquence by the vitality of Armador, Sybilla, and even the Monk.

Hieronymus's very real anguish, metaphysical more than "existential," continues to reach spectators and readers who find him hard to believe as a flesh-and-blood human being. Like Ghelderode, Hieronymus may well have been born onto the wrong planet, seeking a measure of security that, on planet Earth, is rarely to be found after birth. Threatened and eventually betrayed by the Monk, presumably God's earthly representative, Hieronymus proceeds toward the unknown, lulled, like many more credible mortals, into a false sense of security nourished by illusions held well into middle age.

Considered both as play and as document, *Red Magic* shows that Ghelderode had already learned much from his years with the VVT, even as he had disdained to watch over the production of his plays. The action of *Red Magic* is tightly condensed, well able to hold the attention of the average spectator. Only one stage set is needed, and there are only six main characters, plus extras, to be cast. The character of Hieronymus, however, poses several real problems that are not easily surmounted. Hieronymus's soliloquies occupy nearly one-third of the text as printed; even those actors accustomed to playing Shakespeare's *Hamlet* in the title role would find it hard to maintain the breath and force, let alone the memory and command of lines, to play the role of Hieronymus as Ghelderode appears to have intended. Early productions of *Red Magic* tended to taper off toward the end for precisely that reason. In 1971 a production prepared for French television (not broadcast until 1973) was deliberately edited in "tapered" fashion, with the later soliloquies all but suppressed (see Beyen 1974, 61-62). Notwithstanding, *Red Magic* remains among Ghelderode's best-known and most frequently anthologized plays.

Le Siège d'Ostende

Left to his own devices in his attic office, Ghelderode continued to write dramatic scripts at a prodigious rate in the early 1930s, with many scripts later deemed "disposable" by either the author or his critics. In 1933, however, he managed to turn out one true "masterpiece" which, however impossible to produce, began to attract favorable attention well before it appeared in print in 1980, nearly 20 years after Ghelderode's death. Initially planned and executed as homage to the Anglo-Belgian painter James Ensor (1860-1949), *Le Siège d'Ostende* (The Siege of Ostend), subtitled "A Military Epic for Marionettes," contains some of Ghelderode's most expressively poetic prose, together with some of his most memorable conceits.

Liberally "borrowed" from an episode in Flemish history, the plot and setting of *Le Siège d'Ostende* concern an invasion of the

Flemish city by Spanish forces. Sir Jaime l'Ostendais, chosen to take charge of defending the city, is a supposed ancestor of James Ensor and is closely modeled on Ensor. Commanding the Spanish army based in Brussels (waggishly called "Brisselles" in the script) is one Duke Albert, whose duchess (*dussèche*) Isabella goads him on to victory by refusing to change her underwear (*chemyse*) until Ostend has been taken. Sexual and scatological humor abounds, as does biting satire of war, politics, nobility and the clergy. If performed, the action – divided into 19 scenes with nearly 50 characters – would last for approximately two hours. To Ghelderode's disappointment, the aging Ensor was less than honored by the "tribute" offered to him, and Ghelderode in time abandoned whatever further plans he might have had for the script. In retrospect, however, the writing of *Le Siège d'Ostende* seems to have served Ghelderode well in the development of his verbal and scenic talents – talents soon to be exercised again in such plays as *La Balade du grand macabre* (Death Takes a Stroll; 1934) and *La Farce des ténébreux* (The Farce of the Dark Band; 1936).

Lord Halewyn

During his years with the VVT Ghelderode had considered writing a stage version of the Halewijn (or Halewyn) legend, a Flemish folk tale similar in theme and content to that of Bluebeard. At the time, however, another, lesser-known playwright claimed priority rights to the material, and Ghelderode would not begin work on his own version until 1933, having proposed the play as a radio project several months earlier.

A superior example of early radio drama, *Lord Halewyn* recounts the life and death of the title character, a nobleman whose lust for nubile virgins inevitably results in murder. As in the original legend, Halewyn will meet his match in the young countess Purmelende, arguably the one woman who could truly satisfy him. Like Halewyn, Purmelende is haunted by strange needs and voices. As she deliberately rides off in search of Halewyn, she fully expects to meet death as have seven young maidens before her. At the "moment of truth," however, Purmelende awakens as if from a trance and severs Halewyn's head from his body with the sword that he had planned to use on her. Welcomed as a heroine on returning to her father's castle, Purmelende pours out her tale of ecstasy and death, Halewyn's name on her lips as she in turn suddenly dies, her heart "broken" by an excess of emotion.

As befits a play written for radio performance, the action of *Lord Halewyn* is narrated rather than portrayed. The text, however, has proved sufficiently tempting to actors and directors that the play has been staged more than once, with predictably ambiguous results; the actors, indeed, have little more to do than stand in place reciting their lines, more monologue than dialogue. The tale, however, is extremely well retold by Ghelderode, for whom the intermingled themes of sex and death were becoming something of a trademark.

By 1934, when he completed the manuscript of *Lord Halewyn*, Ghelderode was already well-launched on two other projects that would soon come to fruition as *La Balade du grand macabre* and *Miss Jairus*. The former effort seems to have offered Ghelderode some measure of recreation and respite while he worked with the "Jairus" material that he claims to have been haunted by since childhood (see Beyen 1974, 58). Although Death figures prominently in both plays, the portrayal of Nekrozotar in *La Balade du grand macabre* allows for a lightness of touch and tone that is quite absent from Ghelderode's brooding exploration of death and dying in *Miss Jairus*.

La Balade du grand macabre

Earlier in 1933, presumably inspired by figures portrayed on an old tapestry, Ghelderode had composed *Adrian et Jusémina*, a pastoral "diversion" resembling a ballet with dialogue. The title characters and soon to be lovers are shepherd and shepherdess. The names Adrian and Jusémina would be retained to designate the "archetypal" lovers in *La Balade du grand macabre*, although the characters are no longer presented as shepherds. Once again, however, Ghelderode has clearly drawn his inspiration from visual models. The setting of *La Balade du grand macabre* is described as "Breugellande," with scenes clearly recalling Brueghel paintings. It is into this rural setting that the Grim Reaper, Nekrozotar, drops from a tree, initially mistaken for a corpse by the local drunkard, Porprenaz ("purple nose"), who has himself climbed a tree to spy on Adrian and Jusémina.

Brandishing a scythe, Nekrozotar proceeds to announce the end of the world, enclosing the young lovers in a tomb and refusing Porprenaz's offer of his own life as a symbolic sacrifice to spare the people of Breugellande. Mounted on the drunkard's back, Nekrozotar then goes about his business, seeking and finding examples of abuse that more than justify his attentions. In a rapid succession of tableaux, characters and spectators will meet the henpecked astrologer Videbolle ("empty-head"), forced to dress as a woman while his insatiable wife, Salivaine, quite literally wears the pants, smoking a pipe as well. They will also meet the portly, benign Prince Goulave of Breugellande, whose ministers bore him to distraction by advising him to govern badly.

Notwithstanding the acknowledged debt to Brueghel, *La Balade du grand macabre* derives also from *Le Siège d'Ostende*, as from Ghelderode's earlier experiments with puppet theater. Here, however, the scenes and characters are expressly conceived for performance by human actors rather than puppets, convincingly capturing the tone and spirit of such late-medieval farces as *Pierre Pathelin* and *The Tub/La Farce du cuvier*. The latter play, in particular, looms large over Ghelderode's portrayal of Videbolle's troubled life with the salivating Salivaine, who forces him to choose between making love and getting flogged. Videbolle, whose astrological researches have foretold the end of the world, can hardly wait for the event and, in fact, has often prayed for death in order to get away from his shrew of a wife. Salivaine in turn prays to Venus for satisfaction, complaining that her first husband was no better in bed than Videbolle.

When Porprenaz arrives at his friend Videbolle's house bearing Nekrozotar on his back, Videbolle welcomes them with open arms, quite ready to be the first to die. Not so, says Nekrozotar; he will be among the last, because he deserves to witness the "purification" process that is soon to follow. Salivaine, asleep and dreaming, continues to cry out for satisfaction. Nekrozotar, addressing her by name, seizes Salivaine in a vampirelike embrace and bites her shoulder until she faints. In time it will become clear that Nekrozotar is none other than the maligned first husband of Salivaine, who sent him off years ago in search of a mysterious "red herring."

During the action to follow, rich in movement and "stage business" but in fact very tightly constructed, Videbolle, Porprenaz, and Nekrozotar will proceed about the latter's mission; Prince Goulave, who at first hides under a table to avoid the Grim Reaper, looks on with increasing admiration as his principality is purged of its least savory inhabitants. As Goulave will observe, the people in question die not from Nekrozotar's actions but rather from their own fear of what is about to happen. Gluttons, for example, have choked on their food, and misers have swallowed their money in a vain attempt to take it with them. Salivaine, however, remains alive to face a settling of scores, as do the ministers Aspiquet and Basiliquet. After Salivaine, held in place by three old soldiers who have also been spared, has received a ritual flogging at the hands of Videbolle, the two ministers stand revealed as her lovers, taking turns for her dubious affections. It is in fact none other than Salivaine who is responsible for the repressive government forced on Goulave by Aspiquet and Basiliquet, who compete in trying to please her.

In a climactic scene anticipating the end of Ionesco's *Bald Soprano*, Salivaine and her two "lovers" will trade insults and accusations, taking the art of name-calling to new extremes. As order is restored to Breugellande, the three will be left alive as a negative example, kept in a cage to yell and scream at one another for all eternity, or at least for the foreseeable future. Nekrozotar, his mission accomplished, at last feels free to die. As Porprenaz and Videbolle prepare to bury him, the lovers Adrian and Jusémina emerge from the tomb very much alive yet totally unaware of what has been going on around them. The continuity of life in Breugellande is thus assured, the couple signifying renewal and fertility as Videbolle and Proprenaz join hands with Goulave, their newly liberated and enlightened monarch, to celebrate the future.

Delicately (and not always successfully) balanced between fantasy and farce, *La Balade du grand macabre* remained unperformed for nearly 20 years after its composition. Its "ideal" audience would seem to be one already familiar with the twists and turns of Ghelderode's theatrical expression. Even then, in 1953, the recurrent theme and conceit of the "red herring," often mentioned but never seen, continued to pose problems for actors, director, and potentially for spectators. According to Beyen (1974, 75), Ghelderode agreed to sharpen or develop the theme in a revised acting script but in fact never managed to do so. Critics, meanwhile, continued to ponder the symbol on the basis of textual references. For Nekrozotar, the "red herring," once compared to the Holy Spirit, represents the philosopher's quest for the ideal or the absolute. Salivaine, however, quite obviously sees the herring as a phallic symbol, the idealized fulfillment of her insatiable and tyrannical lusts. Such conflicting views of the mythical, even mystical, fish lie at the heart of the "battle of the sexes" embedded in the dialogue. Postwar reviewers, however, seem to have had relatively little difficulty making sense of such references. More than one critic, in 1953, saw *La Balade du grand macabre* as derivative of the connubial farce in the works of Aristophanes, and badly derivative at that.

Other critics, meanwhile, saw in *La Balade du grand macabre* a correction or revision of the negative view of politics espoused in *Barabbas* and in *Pantagleize*. Arguably, however, the setting of *La Balade du grand macabre* is fantastic from the start, an imaginary land harking back, through Goulave's yearnings, to an even more fantastic state of almost prelapsarian perfection, without strife and, perhaps most important, without women. For Beyen (1974, 77), the triumphant, seemingly affirmative final scene of *La Balade du grand macabre* has less to do with brotherhood, as some critics have supposed, than with male bonding, as Porprenaz celebrates the new-found freedom of both Videbolle (from Salivaine) and Goulave (from his ministers). Seen from such a perspective, *La Balade du grand macabre* falls far short of contradicting Ghelderode's earlier views on society and politics. Quite to the contrary, the play emerges as a baroque parable on the intertwined fortunes of politics and sex, either one of which would suffice to render a harmonious society quite impossible indeed.

Women, seldom treated kindly in Ghelderode's dramatic universe, take perhaps their strongest beating – figuratively as well as literally – in *La Balade du grand macabre*. Salivaine, her ugliness underscored by her predilection for masculine dress and mannerisms, is further characterized as cruel and oversexed. If the various images throughout the play are to be taken at face value, Salivaine's sex drive has ruined not only the lives of both of her husbands but also the peaceful society of Breugellande, thanks to her manipulation of the "statesmen" Aspiquet and Basiliquet. Significantly, Salivaine is treated throughout the play as a representative "daughter" of Eve, whose creation gave rise also to the invention of the rod and the whip. The only other female character portrayed is young Jusémina, whose coy words to Adrian hint at fickleness. For want of a better specimen of female humanity, Jusémina will simply have to suffice in order to assure the perpetuation of the human race.

Apart from the negative portrayal of women, a major problem with *La Balade du grand macabre* resides in the shifting role of Nekrozotar, who enters the action as a fearsome, other-worldly Grim Reaper figure only to leave it as yet another failed, henpecked "philosopher" who, sensing the approach of his death, has returned to his homeland on a final mission of "mercy." The resulting changes in tone remain hard to manage in performance, given the need for maintaining the rhythm of physical and verbal farce. Ideally, productions of *La Balade du grand macabre* should accentuate the visual and verbal "distractions" provided by the author, moving fast enough that spectators have little or no time to reflect on the more incongruous aspects of the plot.

Reduced to human scale, Nekrozotar memorably demonstrates the "human" side of death when his victims in fact die of fright, having feared life as much as they fear death. For Ghelderode, such a "demystification" of death helped to defer the more fearsome aspects of his next project, *Miss Jairus*, planned as early as 1929 but with roots reaching back into his earliest childhood. In the Interviews Ghelderode would recall hearing his mother tell of a girl nearly buried alive during the 1870s; although rescued from the grave, the girl would remain in a trancelike, other-worldly state until her actual physical death some years later. The premise of deferred death, recalling the biblical tales of Jairus's daughter and of Lazarus, had continued to grow and develop in Ghelderode's mind even as he seems to have procrastinated in committing his thoughts and feelings to paper. Finally, having "buried" Nekrozotar and temporarily exorcised his own demons, the still-young playwright began work on *Miss Jairus* during the fall of 1934, just one day after finishing *La Balade du grand macabre*.

Miss Jairus

Among the best-known and most frequently discussed of Ghelderode's plays, *Miss Jairus* is set during the late Middle Ages in the ancient city of Bruges. As their daughter Blandine lies on her deathbed, Jairus and his wife, otherwise unnamed, await the inevitable attended by such hangers-on as a witch, a doctor, a priest, professional mourners, and a cabinetmaker who boasts of his skill at constructing coffins. Jairus, ineffectual yet given to histrionics, searches in vain for the proper words and tone for such a crucial moment in his life. Also present, and greatly mistrusted by the other characters, is a mysterious *thaumaturge* (witch doctor) known only as Le Roux ("the redhead"), to whom Ghelderode has assigned, however incongrously, certain Christ-like attributes. Le Roux, it seems, has been summoned by Blandine's fiancé, Jacquelin, who, alone among those present, refuses to accept the fact of the young woman's impending death. In time Le Roux reluctantly agrees to work a miracle out of respect for Jacquelin's faith. He takes care, however, to warn both parents and fiancé that they will come to regret his action and, over time, to hate him for what he has done.

Resuscitated, Blandine awakens in a kind of trance, refusing Jacquelin's attentions and demanding to be left alone. Soon a strange, shrouded figure appears in the doorway to announce that he and Blandine will both die come springtime, some six months later. Dismissing Jacquelin from her presence, Blandine joins the stranger in an eerie, erotic dialogue mixing references to love, lust, and a common desire for death. The two are about to embrace when Jacquelin returns, brandishing a knife. Before long, however, he decides that both Blandine and the stranger are more dead than alive and leaves them alone. As the stranger makes good his escape, promising Blandine that they shall soon meet again, Blandine addresses him as Lazarus.

The fourth and final act of *Miss Jairus* takes place on Good Friday, as the people of Bruges prepare for the ritual execution of three "heretics," including Le Roux. Blandine, deceptively calm at first, breaks into a strangely disjointed monologue as soon as she is left alone. Her speech, anticipating Lucky's monologue in Beckett's *Waiting for Godot*, introduces the play's true climax. When the town crier arrives to announce the death of Lazarus, Blandine asks that her own name be added to the list; she then proceeds to die, her last breath coinciding with that of Le Roux – who dies in the arms of the witch Mankabena, who may or may not be his mother. Jacquelin, returning to close Blandine's eyelids, appears to have undergone some kind of conversion experience and announces his imminent departure to spread the word. Blandine's parents, meanwhile, remain quite as bewildered as ever.

Among the more perplexing, if oddly fascinating, of Ghelderode's published plays, *Miss Jairus* would not be performed until 1949, amid the outbreak of Acute Ghelderoditis on the Paris stage. The play depended on an audience familiar with Ghelderode's work and its characteristic themes, but even such seasoned spectators were baffled by the mixture of sublime and grotesque elements, together with unexplained and seemingly gratuitous references to the New Testament. The three "paid mourners" in particular – three old women all named Marieke who carry onions to induce weeping and whose speech is a curious mixture of French, Dutch, and Latin – struck a discordant note with many observers, as did the ambiguous portrayal of Le Roux, seen by some as a parody of Christ. As with the first performances of *La Balade du grand macabre* some four years later, the irreducible Flemishness of Ghelderode's expression worked at cross-purposes with his total mastery of French poetic prose to keep Paris audiences at bay. Subsequent productions, both within and outside France, took liberties with Ghelderode's original instructions as to costumes and staging, usually in order to accentuate the "romantic appeal" of death embodied in Blandine and in Lazarus.

D'un diable qui prêcha merveilles

Soon after completing *Miss Jairus* Ghelderode continued work on *Sortie de l'acteur*, begun as early as 1933 although back-dated to 1930, the date of Renaat Verheyen's early death. Late in 1935 he began work on a curious text to be known as *D'un diable qui prêcha merveilles* (Of a Devil Who Preached Marvels), designated, as was *Le Siège d'Ostende*, as a play for puppets. Roland Beyen is careful to point out, however, that by the mid-1930s the "puppet" designation had come to hold a somewhat different meaning for

Ghelderode than it had during the 1920s when he actually rehearsed his scripts with marionettes. Beginning with *Le Siège d'Ostende*, the term had come to designate a kind of closet drama or reader's theater uniquely tailored to Ghelderode's own needs without regard for the specific demands of the stage. In the case of *D'un diable*, creative license permitted Ghelderode to invent approximately two dozen characters, involving them in one of his longest and most convoluted scripts.

Set in "Breugelmonde," the action of *D'un diable* recalls that of *La Balade du grand macabre* as well as *Miss Jairus* and *Le Siège d'Ostende*. The scene opens with the lamentations of the sorceress and beggar Fergerite, abandoned by her demon lover Capricant. The town of Breugelmonde, recalling both the Breugellande of *La Balade du grand macabre* and the Bruges of *Miss Jairus*, soon erupts into widespread panic as word travels that the Pope himself has sent an emissary to mend the people's ways. Corruption runs rampant, embodied in such colorful characters as the gluttonous, profane Bishop Bredemaag and the seductive Abbess Didyme, who is about to compound the sin of fornication by attempting an abortion.

Most of the action to follow, divided into three acts, revolves around a case of mistaken identity: Capricant, egged on by his former mistress, Fergerite, impersonates the dreaded monk Bashuiljus, preaching a "sermon" that, in effect, exhorts the townsfolk to remain just as they are. The Pope, he claims, has been misinformed of their activities by inhabitants of rival villages envious of Breugelmonde's prosperity. When the real Bashuiljus at last appears, Capricant gains his confidence by passing himself off as Breugelmonde's purest and most virtuous soul. At the end of the play Capricant has persuaded the monk to leave with him for Rome, where both will be canonized. Life in Breugelmonde will continue just as before, while Capricant will in fact lead the unsuspecting Bashuiljus off to Hell, where he presumably belongs.

Despite rich lyrical and scenic possibilities similar to those of other Ghelderode plays written around the same time, *D'un diable qui prêcha merveilles* remains more often read than performed, notable mainly for its elaboration of Ghelderode's characteristic themes. As in *La Balade du grand macabre*, the intrusion of an other-worldly character serves to reaffirm, albeit in a warped way, the lusty joys of living. The late-medieval setting, meanwhile, provides just enough exoticism to blunt the sharpest edges of Ghelderode's anticlerical satire. Still, the liberal use of long-winded speeches – Capricant's bogus "sermon," for example, occupies the entire second act – tends to work against the text's playability.

Le Farce des ténébreux

Ghelderode's subsequent effort, *La Farce des ténébreux* (The Farce of the Dark Band) is written in much the same vein as its predecessor, denouncing hypocrisy and exhorting the lusty enjoyment of life's transitory pleasures. For once, however, Ghelderode's characteristic anticlericalism is all but absent. He was saving his next full assault on the clergy for *Chronicles of Hell*, to be written the following year. Reminiscent of Baudelaire's prose poem "Laquelle est la vraie?" ("Which One Is for Real?"). The play opens with the monumental grief of one Fernand d'Abcaude, pining away after the sudden death of his fiancée, Azurine. Fernand's servants, including the physician Mops, have tired of their employer's sense of gloom and doom and will stop at nothing to lighten his mood.

With the help of a friend, the actress Emmanuèle, the servants stage an apparition of Azurine's ghostly remains, after which "Azurine" presents Fernand with her maggot-covered heart as a memento. Fernand, deep as ever in despair, fails to get the message, whereupon the conspirators, now including Emmanuèle, proceed to hatch an even bolder scheme. The play's second act takes place in the local bordello, where a most reluctant Fernand has been invited to attend a perverse "memorial service" for one Putrégina, "queen of whores." The other guests, first seen wearing masks, are the "dark band" of the play's title, a "brotherhood" of Putrégina's former customers that includes some of the town's most prominent inhabitants. As the service proceeds, the late prostitute's clothing and other relics are displayed for veneration. It is left to Fernand to unveil the dead woman's statue and thus to discover the true identity of his beloved Azurine. Emmanuèle comes quickly to the rescue, inviting the thunderstruck Fernand to dance with her as the curtain falls.

The third act of *La Farce des ténébreux* takes place, as did the first, in Fernand's room, where the valet Ludion will in time explain to Fernand that what he has recently experienced was no nightmare, but the truth. Pressed for details, Ludion will recall numerous instances of Azurine's lascivity, willfully inviting punishment from his master as he explains that all women are alike and that Fernand would no doubt have been cuckolded in marriage. Left to his own devices, Fernand repeatedly stabs the full-length portrait of Azurine that he has kept in her memory. When Emmanuèle returns, again playing the role of the shrouded Azurine, Fernand continues his interrogation, in time asking the young woman her true identity and profession. When Fernand recoils in horror at the presence of an actress in his house – at a time when actors are deemed unworthy of the sacraments or of Christian burial – Emmanuèle further admits to being a prostitute as well, with Azurine/Putrégina as her role model.

Faced with Fernand's indignation, Emmanuèle is about to leave when Fernand calls her back for further questioning: Why did she play the role of the dead Azurine? For the money, she replies, but also to cure Fernand of his disease, virginity. Patiently, she explains to an astonished Fernand that his rectitude has made him a laughingstock of the community, and that his honor depends on proof of his virility. In a reversal of traditional roles, Emmanuèle then drags a protesting Fernand offstage, presumably into an alcove where she proceeds to undress and seduce him, to the great delight of his entourage. *La Farce des ténébreux* thus comes to an end on a somewhat more disquieting note than Ghelderode seems to have intended. Perhaps, as certain of his critics suggest, Ghelderode unwittingly projected onto his main character some of his own anxieties about women, sex, and death. In any case, his portrayal of the grieving Fernand is shot through with ambiguities that tend to work against the mourner's ribald "liberation" in the final scene.

As developed throughout the action of *La Farce des ténébreux*, Fernand d'Abcaude is simply too complex a character to be set free from his inhibitions (or are they moral convictions?) in the manner described. The "pillars of the community" who comprise the "dark band" may well be hypocrites, but Fernand himself is not. As presented and developed, Fernand is either a pious man of principle or a case of arrested development. Perhaps, indeed, he is both at once – a dreamer truly obsessed with an ideal of purity equally binding on himself and on the woman he loves. His "liberation" therefore strikes something of a false note, as if Fernand were being punished for his chastity with what amounts to an act of rape.

Owing no doubt to ambiguities in the portrayal of Fernand, *La Farce des ténébreux* was among the last of Ghelderode's efforts to be staged during the "epidemic" of Acute Ghelderoditis in Paris. Jean-Louis Barrault, seldom daunted by the difficulties of a dramatic text, nonetheless abandoned plans to mount the play during the 1950-51 season at the Théâtre Marigny, having already had sets built and posters printed. The sets, constructed by Félix Labisse, were finally used in November 1952 when Georges Vitaly staged the play at the Grand Guignol, taking considerable liberties with the text in order to render it playable as comedy. Even so, the production was less than a rousing success, and nearly two decades would pass before a second attempt at production, in Brussels in 1970.

By 1936 Ghelderode's health was beginning to fail him, which may or may not help to account for the increasingly morbid concerns to be found in his plays of the period. True, the mingled themes of sex and death had characterized most of his plays from *Red Magic* onward; still, the paralyzing scruples – or inhibitions – of Fernand in *La Farce des ténébreux* sound a new, discomfiting note in Ghelderode's dramatic canon. Despite the author's avowed intentions, there is little or nothing to celebrate in Fernand's eventual "destiny." The affirmative spirit that came to Ghelderode's rescue in such efforts as *La Balade du grand macabre* somehow appears to have deserted him, replaced by strong intimations of mortality, sterility, and man's – or, more frequently, woman's – inhumanity to man.

Hop, Signor!

Soon after completing *La Farce des ténébreux* in July 1936, Ghelderode turned his attention to a project first outlined some 18 months earlier and loosely based, like *Lord Halewyn*, on folklore. The result, known even in translation as *Hop, Signor!*, would in time become one of the author's most notorious and frequently reprinted plays, even as the themes and tone expressed would, as in the case of *La Farce des ténébreux*, assure relatively few productions, at least in France.

Having attempted a comic treatment of lust and inhibition in *La Farce des ténébreux*, Ghelderode in *Hop, Signor!* would revisit the same themes in a tone rather delicately balanced between tragedy and melodrama yet partaking of the scenic vigor associated with *Red Magic*. If the earlier play, at least in intent, constituted an attack on hypocrisy, *Hop, Signor!* goes even deeper into perceived human nature to show the basic incompatibility of the sexes – a perennial problem to which death would appear the only possible solution.

Based on the well-documented medieval punishment (or torture) of tossing an offender in a blanket or tarpaulin to break his bones – a tradition recalled down to the present day in the children's game known in Dutch as *Opsignoorke* and played with a doll – *Hop, Signor!* centers on the troubled career and marriage of the sculptor Juréal, deformed and aging, who hides his insecurities beneath a superficial arrogance that has earned him the sobriquet of Signor, or "milord." In constructing the play Ghelderode borrowed from yet another folkloric/historical source to present as Juréal's wife one Marguerite Harstein, executed for witchcraft during the sixteenth century.

Unable either to adapt his art to changing tastes or to consummate his marriage to the alluring, demanding Marguerite, Juréal easily falls prey to the blandishments of Helgar and Adorno, two handsome young noblemen who curry favor with him in hopes of getting closer to his wife. Marguerite, while expressing nothing but contempt for her husband and ridiculing his attempts to practice the manly art of fencing, keeps her two admirers at bay by playing them off against each other. As will soon become clear, Marguerite's inhibitions, similar to those of Purmelende in *Lord Halewyn*, are hardly less severe than those of her unfortunate spouse. Notwithstanding, her speech and actions exude a strong sexuality that helps to precipitate the play's dramatic, even tragic, action.

When Juréal, as proud as he is insecure, invites Marguerite to accompany him to a public procession in order to keep up appearances or at least to save face, Marguerite brutally informs him that there are no appearances to be kept up and no face to save. Everyone knows that he is virile only in his arms, she says, and only for the humble craft of carving tombstones. If only she were so inclined, she adds, she would already have betrayed him many times over. His pride mortally wounded, Juréal flies into an impotent rage, heaving an enormous carved stone that nearly hits and kills the monk Dom Pilar, who has been spying on him for Helgar and Adorno.

Close kin to the monk in *Red Magic*, as to the corrupt clergy in the forthcoming *Chronicles of Hell*, Dom Pilar plays both ends against the middle by arousing Juréal's jealous anger and then attempting, unsuccessfully, to receive Marguerite's confession. Juréal, meanwhile, alerted by the two dwarfs who work for him that the play being performed in the public square has to do with cuckoldry, takes the matter personally and goes off to avenge his honor, brandishing a sword. The focus then shifts to a curious scene between Marguerite and the executioner Larose, alternately described as strongly built, athletic, and catlike, who chews on an eponymous rose stem as others might chew on a blade of grass. Their dialogue and interaction is intensely sensual, even as both parties profess their chastity. Oddly uninhibited in the presence of Larose, Marguerite admits to a kind of ecstasy when she watches his public beheadings, to which Larose evasively replies that many women become pregnant after watching him at work.

Soon thereafter curious sounds and silences announce the agony and death of Juréal, who has been tossed in a blanket and then dropped fatally to the ground when someone let go of the blanket. Marguerite, a less-than-bereaved widow, refuses to sign the cross on her late husband's forehead when Dom Pilar bids her to do so. She also asks that the corpse continue to be tossed in the air as it is carried out of town. Unable to attract Larose, who has conveniently made himself scarce, Marguerite then summons her two noble admirers, provocatively offering herself to the one who will claim greater responsibility for her husband's death.

As Marguerite leaves to wait in her room for her "deliverer," the two noblemen – identified by Dom Pilar as foreign spies – draw swords as they vie for the honor just offered to them by Juréal's widow. Adorno wins the duel and flees, leaving the dying Helgar to be comforted by Marguerite who, promising to love him "for the rest of his life," offers to close his mortal wound with her lips. Dom Pilar then emerges from yet another hiding place. Marguerite, covered in Helgar's blood, beside herself with anger and desire, presents one bare breast to the astonished Dom Pilar, offering to stuff it down his throat as she gives herself to the most monstrous bidder – himself. Pilar, unwillingly seized by lust, denounces Marguerite as possessed by the Devil, murmuring the *Agnus Dei* as he slips from her embrace onto the ground, covering his face. Marguerite is still trying to seduce the monk when the dwarfs reappear, closely followed by the executioner Larose. In the sudden presence of Larose, Marguerite falls into a kind of stupor from which she will not awaken even when denounced by townsfolk and authorities for the violent deaths of Juréal and Helgar. Larose then leads her off to the only "consummation" in which either of them might find satisfaction, leaving the last words to the two dwarfs, Mèche ("Wick") and Suif ("Tallow") whose antics opened the play. Mocking the theater itself, Tallow observes that it is not only on the stage where several people die in one day. When Wick asks him if it is right to mourn a dead man, Tallow replies that it would be better to mourn him at birth, on his entry into this miserable world. The play then ends with the two dwarfs, ugly and deformed like their late master, tossing in a blanket a broken puppet dressed in Juréal's clothes, chanting "Hop, Signor!" as the puppet rises and falls.

Rich in sight and sound, *Hop, Signor!* as written is every bit as arresting as *Red Magic* and even more tightly constructed, hardly longer than the traditional one-act play. Having uncharacteristically indulged himself in prolixity and verbosity with such efforts as *La Balade du grand macabre* and *La Farce des ténébreux*, Ghelderode in *Hop, Signor!* returned to the procedure first used to advantage in *Escurial*, allowing theme and subject matter to determine length and form instead of tailoring both to fit the perceived demands of traditional drama. The result is extremely stageworthy. If *Hop, Signor!* is less frequently performed than *Escurial* or *Red Magic*, this has less to do with its construction than with the audacity of its themes and the negations implied in its conclusion. It is likely, too, that many would-be directors or performers have shied away from the text because of what it seems to reveal about the author.

As Beyen observes, seldom did Ghelderode write himself into a text so visibly as he did in preparing and developing the character of Juréal, a sexual and social misfit whose art is anchored in the past and hopelessly out of touch with the prevailing taste. Denied the contrived, implausibly "happy" fate reserved for Fernand d'Abcaude, Juréal can only fall victim to an implacably hostile universe made even more hostile by the presence of his fellow mortals. Citing a letter written at the time by Ghelderode to a friend, the engraver Jac Boonen, Beyen shows that Ghelderode sought in *Hop, Signor!* to show the cruelty of man that religions have not only been unable to correct but have in fact tended to cultivate (Beyen 1974, 103).

Dom Pilar, to be sure, does considerably more harm than good, as do most clerics in Ghelderode's dramatic canon. He is, however, only a part of the problem so graphically set forth in *Hop, Signor!* Cruelty, it would seem, is embedded in the nature of the sexes, doomed to incompatibility by conflicting needs and demands. In Marguerite Harstein Ghelderode has managed to combine elements of Purmelende, Salivaine, and the charming but two-faced Azurine/Putrégina to provide his most disquieting, even unnerving, portrait of woman. Undeniably attractive, as Salivaine surely is not, Marguerite denounces Juréal for his impotence even as she proclaims her own disinclination toward extramarital affairs, and her continued "baiting" of the two young noblemen ends, not surprisingly, in Helgar's death. No man, it seems, can provide the ecstasy toward which her sexuality tends – a longing that can be satisfied only in her death at the hands of the equally "virginal" Larose, who bears, moreover, a feminine name.

Although infrequently staged since its first production (in French) in Brussels in 1942, *Hop, Signor!* remains among the most frequently read and discussed of all of Ghelderode's plays, notable, like *Escurial*, for its efficiency and economy of expression. Such autobiographical (or autopsychological) overtones as there may be are quite literally upstaged by the utter bleakness of the play's apparent "message," as by the author's scathing portrayal of the possible interactions among life, death, sex and art.

Chronicles of Hell

Once he had, in a sense, dramatized his nagging distrust of women and, indeed, of the reproductive process itself, Ghelderode returned with a vengeance to yet another of his bêtes noires with *Chronicles of Hell*, in which all of the male characters are members of the Roman Catholic clergy. If, as his written statement to Jac Boonen implies, Ghelderode saw religion as fostering mankind's innate cruelty, he arguably set out to prove as much in his evocation of riot and celebration surrounding the death of a bishop murdered with a poisoned communion wafer.

Although dated 1929 in the Gallimard edition of Ghelderode's collected plays, *Chronicles of Hell* would appear, in Beyen's chronology, to have been composed, for the most part, during the fall of 1936 and the fall of 1937. While Ghelderode might well have framed or outlined the play's basic premise toward the end of the preceding decade, his technique and style tend to support, in Beyen's view, the documentary evidence favoring the later date (Beyen 1974, 104).

Chronicles of Hell begins in Flanders with an unseen crowd of worshipers clamoring to view the remains of the just-deceased Bishop Jan in Eremo of Lapideopolis, whom they revere as a saint. The bishop's fellow clergymen, meanwhile, indulge themselves in food and drink to celebrate their liberation from the bishop's strict rule. Six riotous scenes bordering on farce precede the arrival of the allusively named Sodomati, secretary to the papal nuncio. In Sodomati's presence, the auxiliary bishop, Simon Laquedeem, identified as a converted Jew, begins to eulogize the deceased cleric's life and career. Suddenly, amid thunder and lightning, Jan in Eremo rises from his deathbed brandishing his episcopal staff. All the clerics flee except for Laquedeem, who attacks the "dead man" with an ax. A brief struggle finds the ax in the hands of Bishop Jan, who is about to strike back when he "freezes" as if entranced, having recognized the aged servant Véneranda as his mother.

The bishop then tries to speak but cannot produce audible sound. When he points toward his throat, the old woman orders him to his knees and pulls from his throat a foreign object that turns out to be the poisoned Host. Faced with her son's abiding anger, Véneranda further orders him to pardon those who have sinned against him if he expects to be pardoned himself, then slaps him across the face when he is slow to respond, exhorting him to obey his mother. A dutiful son once more, the septuagenarian bishop, no doubt already dead, unclenches his fist to form the upraised palm of benediction. Véneranda then helps him back to his deathbed, where he can die in peace, the fact of his murder having been revealed.

Sure at last that his arch-enemy is dead, Simon Laquedeem, who administered the poison, takes back the wafer from the hands of Sodomati and, announcing Communion, force-feeds it to Véneranda, who predictably falls dead not long thereafter. Once the bishop's body has been removed by a team of "athletic" butchers, the clergymen once again celebrate their deliverance. Since all have eaten and drunk at least their fill, the "celebration" soon degenerates into a paroxysm of scatology, with the priests sniffing each other's backsides like dogs as they indulge in flatulence and defecation. In the final scene Laquedeem squats suggestively before the audience, a fiendish smile on his "rabbinical" face as the curtain falls.

Although devoid of the sexual references that permeate *Hop, Signor!* and *La Farce des ténébreux*, *Chronicles of Hell* proved soon after its initial performances in 1949 to be Ghelderode's most controversial play, at least in France, defying not only good taste but also the ingrained Gallic sense of logic. Even in a country inured to anticlerical sentiment, Ghelderode's all-out attack on the clergy seemed gratuitous at best, offensive at worst, with strong overtones of anti-Semitism in the author's portrayal of Laquedeem, whose name recalls that often assigned to the Wandering Jew of legend (see Blancart-Cassou, 163). Still, the verbal and visual qualities of *Chronicles of Hell* would bring Acute Ghelderoditis to its height on the Parisian stage, assuring a ready, if temporary, audience for a number of Ghelderode's earlier work.

For Jacqueline Blancart-Cassou, *Chronicles of Hell* embodies a type of "solitary laughter" characteristic to Ghelderode's final phase, a grating laughter on the author's part that, by its nature, defies audience participation (168). It is clear in any case that Ghelderode by 1937 was writing increasingly "for himself," perhaps to exorcise his private demons. As in the case of *Hop, Signor!*, it is frequently difficult for an audience to share in the author's projected vision. Indeed, as Beyen has demonstrated, Ghelderode in the late 1930s feared the decline of his dramatic talents along with his health. On the evidence, he doubtless had cause for concern on both counts. Turning increasingly toward composition of the genre fiction to be collected in *Sortilèges*, Ghelderode would complete no more than three plays prior to being "discovered" by the French avant-garde soon after World War II, and only one play thereafter.

Late in 1937, after finishing *Chronicles of Hell*, Ghelderode returned to the general theme of a 1935 radio play to create *La Pie sur le gibet* (Magpie on the Gallows), portraying the arrest and execution of the legendary trickster Tyl Eulenspiegel against the background of an eponymous painting by Brueghel the Elder. *L'Ecole des bouffons* (School for Jesters) was outlined as early as 1937 but not actually written until 1942, after publication of *Sortilèges*. *Le Soleil se couche* (The Sun Sets) recalls the last days of the Hapsburg Emperor Charles V in a manner reminiscent of *Escurial* yet lacking that play's tight construction. Ghelderode was quite literally "played out" by the time he became famous as a dramatist. Acute Ghelderoditis would, however, lead not only to the Ostend Interviews but also to the composition of what turned out to be his final play, *Marie la misérable*.

Marie la misérable

During the summer of 1950 the newly rediscovered Ghelderode received a request from the Belgian community of Woluwé-Saint-Lambert to dramatize the legend of the local martyr Lenneke Mare, the spectacle to be staged outdoors, on the actual site, in June 1952 to commemorate the six-hundred-fiftieth anniversary of her death. Although ill and frail, Ghelderode found the legend quite to his liking and took no more than two days to decide in the affirmative. He would not, however, actually begin work on the script until the fall of 1951, after taping the Ostend Interviews.

As first performed – on schedule – during the summer of 1952, *Marie la misérable* puts the virtuous, virginal Marie La Cluse, in her early thirties and known also as Lenneke Mare, in apposition to the hot-blooded young nobleman Eglon d'Arken, several years her junior, whose unrequited longing for Marie turns gradually to hate. Marie, who devotes her life to the poor and infirm although she has not actually taken the veil, harbors few illusions about men and treats her would-be suitor with candid scorn. He is, she points out, both rich and idle, lacking only the opportunity to prove his manhood in battle. Repeatedly rejected, d'Arken is about to renounce his suit when his jester Rostenduvel ("Red Devil") resolves to avenge his master's honor by "framing" Marie for the theft of a golden goblet belonging to Jean II, duke of Brabant. In time, the young woman is falsely accused, tried, convicted and sentenced to death for the crime, further accused by Rostenduvel of practicing witchcraft. At Marie's execution Rostenduvel is thrown onto the pyre as well, only to be resuscitated in the third and final act, where he exhorts his

master, ostracized by the townsfolk for his part in Marie's death, to
commit suicide.

The priest Adam Gherys, who tried in vain to save Marie's life,
intervenes to show d'Arken that Rostenduvel was no more than an
hallucination. When the duke arrives on the scene, d'Arken begs his
forgiveness, admitting that he conspired in Marie's death out of love
turned to hate, to destroy what he could not have. Marie then
appears in a vision shared by the duke and all the townsfolk, whereupon d'Arken dons the garb of a pilgrim and prepares to leave for
Jerusalem and Rome, accompanied by the mysterious Marie Cantilie,
who may or may not be Marie La Cluse's mother. The action then
ends on a decidedly affirmative note recalling that of Carnival as the
duke drinks from the once-lost golden vessel, exhorting his loyal
subjects to join him in commemorating Marie's exemplary life and
sacrifice.

Among the longest – and wordiest – of Ghelderode's plays,
Marie la misérable, although included in the Gallimard edition of
his plays, is suitable for production only on the premises for which it
was intended, and where it has indeed frequently been revived. In
Beyen's view, however, it is markedly superior in verbal and scenic
quality to the average run of historical pageants and "sound and
light" spectacles commonly performed across Europe (1974, 117).
Despite the necessarily archaic setting and tone, Ghelderode has
managed to create vivid, credible characters who elicit and sustain
the spectator's interest. Given the exemplary nature of the legend,
the "message" of *Marie la misérable* is rather more affirmative than
those to be deduced from Ghelderode's last plays of the 1930s, in
particular, *Hop, Signor!* and *Chronicles of Hell*. Unlike Marguerite
Harstein, whose virginity masks a perverted lust, Marie La Cluse is
presented as a prototypical saint who dies so that Eglon d'Arken and
the other townsfolk might be saved. Unlike Bishop Jan in *Eremo*, she
is thus shown not to have died in vain.

Ghelderode's ingrained pessimism might well have been held in
check by the promise of a check. *Marie la misérable* was, after all,
prepared in response to a commission, and the spectacle was meant
to be somewhat uplifting. It would be misleading, however, to infer
that Ghelderode here perjured himself as he refused to do for the
VVT, when dealing with Barabbas or Saint Francis of Assisi. As in his
earlier plays, the forces of evil are quite evident and credible.

Indeed, it is hard to imagine another author bringing the material to life as convincingly as does Ghelderode. The effort, however, seems to have dealt a final blow to his creative energies even as it rekindled his interest in playwriting. Although new dramatic projects would be announced following the generally favorable reception of *Marie la misérable*, none would be completed.

Ghelderode's "return" to the late Middle Ages and early Renaissance in search of material appears to have assured his place in literary and dramatic history. Had his evolution as a dramatist stopped with his association with the VVT, Ghelderode might well be remembered – if at all – among the few expressionists who wrote in French, with the truly ground-breaking *Escurial* either overlooked or forgotten. By digging deeper into the vein that had produced *Escurial*, Ghelderode during the 1930s developed a singular dramatic voice and style that would resist assimilation into any school or movement, even as Acute Ghelderoditis helped to create a climate favorable to the reception of such Absurdist playwrights as Beckett, Ionesco, and the early Adamov. By the time Acute Ghelderoditis had run its course in the mid-1950s, the best of Ghelderode's plays, including *Red Magic*, *La Balade du grand macabre*, and *Escurial*, had passed into the worldwide dramatic repertory.

Ghelderode, working on his own and for himself, might well have returned to the medieval and renaissance period in search of private demons to exorcise. If so, it might also be argued that the demons finally got the better of him, particularly in *Hop, Signor!* and *Chronicles of Hell*. Although the language and style are forceful, Ghelderode's authorial voice in those two plays veers away from the universal toward the particular and even the personal, making it hard for the spectator or even the actor to take part in the experience portrayed. The universality of his earlier plays, however, continues to assure his place in the international dramatic canon.

Chapter Five

Ghelderode and the Self-Conscious Stage

Writing plays as if by instinct and in time perhaps compulsively, Ghelderode practiced at the expense of preaching. He wrote no theory or criticism of drama, and those few reviews attributed to him reveal little of his attitude toward theater in general. No doubt ill-prepared to discuss his craft in the Ostend Interviews, Ghelderode tended to offer anecdote in place of substance or to direct interviewers to the texts themselves for elucidation. Indeed, the strongest clues to Ghelderode's "philosophy" of drama lie embedded within the texts – most evidently, although not exclusively, in those efforts where the theatre takes itself as subject. Even then, however, one must bear in mind that certain "quotable quotes" are, in fact, lines from a play and do not *necessarily* represent the author's views.

As early as *The Death of Doctor Faust* Ghelderode had experimented with *mise-en-abyme*, which has tempted dramatists since even before Shakespeare. Ghelderode's *Don Juan*, although lacking *mise-en-abyme*, focuses considerable attention on the interplay of illusion and reality essential to the dramatic experience, as does *Escurial* with the feverish exchange of roles between performer/jester and spectator/king. On into the 1930s a number of Ghelderode characters such as Hieronymus in *Red Magic* and Nekrozotar in *La Balade du grand macabre* would seem to be aware of striking poses. It is perhaps no accident that David Grossvogel, whose substantial chapter on Ghelderode first introduced many Americans to this playwright, originally titled his volume *The Self-Conscious Stage in Modern French Drama*. To an even greater degree than the work of most of his contemporaries writing in the French idiom, Ghelderode's plays tend toward the self-referential, calling spectacle and spectator into question even as the action proceeds.

Responding, however belatedly, to the sudden death of the actor
Renaat Verheyen, who had helped bring his early plays to life for the
VVT, Ghelderode around 1933 would begin work on his most "self-
conscious" play to date – *Sortie de l'acteur* – moving beyond a simple *mise-en-abyme* toward a penetrating, poetically conceived
inquiry into the nature of creative and interpretive art. The action
begins with the author Jean-Jacques – the playwright himself in
mocking caricature – trying vainly to correct and animate a troupe of
burnt-out, third-rate actors in rehearsing his latest – and last – play
in the absence of the actor cast in the leading role. When Renatus – named for Verheyen and the only truly talented performer in
the cast – finally arrives at the theater, he is in no condition to
rehearse, having contracted a severe chill while attending a funeral
in a nearby church. Renatus's chill and the funeral will soon take on
metaphysical proportions as he relates both experiences to his part
in Jean-Jacques's play, a role that culminates in his character's death.

As the action proceeds, Renatus's feverish, increasingly halluci-
natory speeches will repeatedly confuse his character's impending
death with his own, holding the demoralized Jean-Jacques somehow
accountable for both. There is too much death in Jean-Jacques's
plays, explains Renatus, and not enough love. It soon develops that
Renatus's character faces execution for having made love to the
Queen, who, transformed into a saint, will plant a kiss of pardon on
the lips of his severed head. (One cannot, incidentally, help but
admire the irony of Ghelderode's self-parody, even as the scene
evokes memories of Oscar Wilde's *Salomé*.) What is more, argues
Renatus, Jean-Jacques's art is downright dangerous, although rather
less so than it might be if it reached a wider audience! Admitting his
own susceptibility to Jean-Jacques's peculiar brand of "contagion,"
transmitted through repeated exposure to his plays, Renatus accuses
the author of having revealed to him his own unhappiness, endemic
to the human condition (3:32-33). Face to face with the comely
actress Armande, cast as the saintly Queen, Renatus consistently con-
fuses the performer with her role, having already lamented to Jean-
Jacques that the Queen's kiss on his dead lips will be the closest he
has ever come to love.

In the sixth and perhaps best-remembered of the Ostend Interviews, Roger Iglésis and Alain Trutat would remind Ghelderode of
Renatus's reproaches to Jean-Jacques in *Sortie l'acteur*, asking him

to account for the priority of death over love in the Ghelderode
canon and the nearly total absence of love. Ghelderode, increasingly
evasive and irascible, denounces the prevalence of sex and "lust" in
mainstream entertainment, arguing that the theater has no business
portraying "normal" human beings and that when it does, they
should be presented in abnormal situations. All the rest, he claims, is
"bourgeois pornography."

There are monsters in his plays, Ghelderode continues, because
there are monsters everywhere, all around us, within us; we are
monsters ourselves and it is pointless to pretend otherwise (*EO*, 173-
74). Even in the heavily edited, published text of the Interviews,
Ghelderode's guarded replies are interspersed with such disclaimers
as *"Ne vous en déplaise . . ."* ("if you don't mind . . .") and *"Sans
rancune"* ("No offense"). Toward the end of the session (and,
apparently, the playwright's patience) Ghelderode would claim not
to have invented out of whole cloth such characters as Purmelende
d'Ostrelande or Marguerite Harstein but to have drawn them par-
tially from life where such creatures do, in fact, exist (*EO*, 180-81).

Ironically, *Sortie de l'acteur* also contains, in brutal counter-
point to Renatus's sufferings, the closest thing to a conventional love
scene to be found in Ghelderode's theater. Against the background
of the actor's delirium, the playwright Jean-Jacques will reach clumsily out to the actress Armande, whom he claims to have admired for
years without finding the courage to declare his feelings. Armande, in
turn, has long since outgrown any penchant she might have had for
the writer who, she claims, has perpetually since ignored her presence in favor of his questionable "art"; she further accuses Jean-
Jacques of having cultivated "morbid tastes" in the impressionable,
now feverish young actor. Armande then storms out of the theater
with Jean-Jacques in pursuit, leaving Renatus to his ravings.

Left to his own devices, Renatus meditates aloud as to the role of
death in the theater: How else can plays end? Rising from his cot, the
actor "exchanges roles" with a mannequin that he dresses in his
own clothes. Moments later, when the prompter Fagot appears,
Renatus will deliberately confuse his friend Fagot as to which is the
ventriloquist and which the dummy. Figuring out the ruse at last,
Fagot will lead Renatus off toward the relative safety of his seedy fur-
nished room.

As the curtain rises on act 2, Renatus, pronounced in extremis by a doctor summoned by Fagot, has been hallucinating lines and scenes from plays in which he has performed. When Jean-Jacques arrives to check on the actor's condition, Fagot at first warns him not to reveal his presence, fearful that the sight or sound of the playwright will hasten the actor's decline. In time, however, Fagot decides that the presence of Jean-Jacques might, in fact, be reassuring. No sooner has the author approached Renatus than Armande comes in, having inquired at the theater about Jean-Jacques's whereabouts. She has apparently changed her mind and is now willing to reciprocate the playwright's attentions. Renatus, sensing the mutual approach of the two would-be lovers as they, in turn, sense the approach of his death, rants and raves in his increasing delirium, with incoherence interspersed with visionary lucidity. Hallucinating the presence of a doctor (to be played by Fagot if visual representation is desired), Renatus goes beyond a listing of his symptoms to imagine his own autopsy and to dictate a fantastic will. Having "bequeathed" his many roles or appearances to the surviving actors, he will have ceased to exist, will he not? Does the doctor exist, or is he an actor too? As author and actress continue their tawdry antiflirtation in the foreground, Renatus leaps out of bed in a final paroxysm and collapses into a chair, where he dies just as members of his troupe arrive with flowers and get-well presents.

In the third and final act, drawn even closer to fantasy than the second, Renatus is buried in a mist-covered cemetery as his fellow actors and Jean-Jacques divide their time between the funeral and a nearby tavern managed by Fagot who, during his checkered career, has served also as sacristan and as pantomime artist. With time, all of the mourners become quite intoxicated, free with their own observations concerning life and death. Armande, shunning Jean-Jacques, claims to be "haunted" by the shade of Renatus, which in fact appears before Jean-Jacques in the play's memorable final scene.

Costumed in death as in life, Renatus, now a ghostly presence, confides to Jean-Jacques that he is fleeing celestial policemen bent on carrying him off to Heaven. The playwright, having begged and received Renatus's pardon for any harm done, will intercede to protect his friend from the fearsome angelic show of force, only to be bludgeoned for his efforts by the commanding angel. In the end it is Renatus who saves Jean-Jacques from further harm by surrendering to his captors, who then push him awkwardly and clumsily up a ladder toward his "ascension." The author, left alone with Fagot, wonders aloud if anyone will ever find the key to the mystery. What key? Fagot wonders aloud in his turn; did Jean-Jacques not know that mystery has no door? (3: 284).

Rich in poetic allusions and conceits, *Sortie de l'acteur* lends itself to many interpretations and speculations about Ghelderode's philosophy of drama, and of life. At the very least, the theater is shown to be as dangerous as it is compelling – at least to certain individuals. On the other hand, it may well be the only possible "key" to a mystery that has no door. The only certainty in life, suggests Ghelderode, is death, and dramatic art is one way, if not the only way, to come to terms with death while one still lives.

Significantly, *Sortie de l'acteur* was Ghelderode's last play – and indeed, his first in several years – to be set in the chronological present. It was also his last dramatic text, with the exception of the commissioned *Marie la misérable*, to be divided into conventional acts and scenes. It is thus a sport in the Ghelderodian canon, representing a deliberate – and temporary – break in the routine that Ghelderode had set for himself during the 1930s. Perhaps, as suggested by internal evidence (see 3: 275), Ghelderode honestly believed while writing *Sortie de l'acteur* that it was to be his last play. In any event, it remains among the more accessible and playable of Ghelderode's mature efforts, providing a useful point of entry into an otherwise bewildering body of dramatic work.

Years later, having for all practical purposes renounced playwriting to prepare and publish the short fiction comprising *Sortilèges*, Ghelderode would return to the subject of self-conscious stagecraft with *L'Ecole des bouffons*, a fast-paced, convulsive work that pushes beyond the apparent self-destructiveness of Renatus and Jean-Jacques toward an even more unsettling conclusion.

Set in a former Flemish convent during the latter half of the sixteenth century, *L'Ecole des bouffons* portrays a class of apprentice court buffoons grown restive under the strict professional standards and iron discipline of their teacher Folial, a mater of the craft, knighted for his talents and service but now aging and ailing. To show the old man what they have learned, the apprentices, all deformed or otherwise ill-favored by nature, have planned an impromptu spectacle that will cause him to drop dead from shock and grief when he sees it.

Using the *mise-en-abyme* to greater effect than in any of his prior efforts, Ghelderode in *L'Ecole des bouffons* has the apprentices reenact with youthful disrespect the personal tragedy that has brought about Folial's decline – the recent death of his beloved daughter. She has either been murdered or killed herself in Spain, as a result of a love triangle involving her, the crown prince, and one of her father's disciples, also known as Folial. Only momentarily fooled by the spectacle of what has spawned his suffering, the old man flies into a towering but far from blind rage, unleashing tremendous power with his whip as he forces the principal "actors" to mount the catafalque that they used for a stage property, there to await certain execution. He then whips the remaining apprentices into prancing around the catafalque like horses in a circus ring. As he has observed, it takes more than that to kill a "pedigree" jester like himself. In the memorable final scene of the long single act, the venerable jester finally reveals to his cowering, whimpering former disciples the secret of the jester's art, of great art, of all lasting art: "CRU-EL-TY!" Cracking his whip into the void, the old man, smiling through his tears, finally turns the whip on himself as the curtain falls on *L'Ecole des bouffons*.

Even more than the crack of Folial's whip, the aging jester's final words, culminating in "cruelty," would reverberate into the perceived void that eventually absorbed Ghelderode's unorthodox approach to theater. By the early 1950s, the same milieu that cultivated Acute Ghelroditis would also have discovered the dramatic theories of Antonin Artaud (1896-1948), who had used the same term in outlining his idealized concept of a "total theatre." "Cruelty" had in fact become something of a buzz word among theater practitioners, and it was not long before Ghelderode's use of the term in *L'Ecole des bouffons* led to confusion of his dramatic practice with the theories first advanced by Artaud some 20 years earlier.

In the Ostend Interviews Ghelderode would disclaim any knowledge of Artaud or his theories until sometime after the composition of *L'Ecole des bouffons*, which he had conveniently back-dated to 1937. As Roland Beyen has pointed out, however, Ghelderode even in 1951 had only the sketchiest concept of Artaud's writings, and might not, indeed, have yet read them (1974, 112). Despite similar terminology and apparent means to a desired end, the practitioner and the theorist remain sharply divided as to what cruelty in the theater is supposed to *prove*. For Artaud, cruelty is somehow liberating, leading toward a kind of "purification" of human nature not unlike the "purgation" prescribed in the Aristotelian canon. For Ghelderode, by contrast, cruelty is, in a sense, both means and end, since no "liberation" or "purification" is possible. His implied aim is simply to tell mankind the truth about itself, at best to strip away the many masks with which "society" seeks to hide or disguise the basic meanness and "cruelty" of the human condition.

Although certain of Ghelderode's plays might well be, and indeed have been, seen as practical illustrations of Artaud's esthetic principles, the two writers are further divided by their approach to language on the stage. Artaud, simultaneously jaded by the logocentrism of French drama of the nineteenth century and intrigued by nonverbal aspects of the Asian theatrical tradition, tended to denigrate and devalue both lyricism and "literature" on the stage. Ghelderode, unversed in the Asian practice yet imbued with the oral tradition of his Flemish ancestors, remained strongly attached to poetic and linguistic values even as he explored the potential resources of space, sound effects, music, color, and the plastic arts in order to enhance elements already present in the projected text.

David Grossvogel, exposing and exploring Ghelderode's work for the benefit of a potentially receptive American audience, devoted considerable attention to Ghelderode's nearly exhaustive use of sight and sound in preparing his texts for the stage. To be sure, Ghelderode – whose *didascalies* (stage directions) might cover a full page and rank among the most voluminous and prescriptive in the history of printed dramatic texts – would more than once come close to realizing the "total theater" propounded by Artaud. Even then, however, language remains firmly rooted at the center of the planned spectacle (see Beyen 1974, 140-41). Finally, it must be noted that the "cruelty" of Ghelderode's dramaturgy, although perhaps most fully articulated in the final speech of *L'Ecole des bouffons* had been present in his plays from the start, culminating in the mid-1930s with *Hop, Signor!* and *Chronicles of Hell*.

If Artaud intended theater to be subversive, so too did Michel de Ghelderode, albeit in different ways and for different reasons. Artaud's theories, although diametrically opposed to those of Bertolt

Brecht, were not without a political agenda, however vaguely defined. The aim of Artaud's "total theater," with its concomitant "cruelty," was the release of elemental human energies that would, in the long run, work toward the advantage of the "masses." Ghelderode, for his part, could not have cared less about the "masses" or the collectivity, whose efforts toward change would, as in *Pantagleize*, tend inevitably toward more of the same, given the basic flaws in human nature.

If Ghelderode practiced subversion it was quite without agenda, aimed first and only at releasing his own elemental human energy – an energy focused and perhaps distorted by the immediate specter of death. Committed only to art, with a jaundiced eye further trained by repeated exposure to the images produced by Bosch, Brueghel, Velázquez, Goya, and Ensor, he sought mainly to express through merged media the abiding spectacle of human cruelty and meanness, the monsters that lurk all around us and within us. Like the aging Folial, who has produced laughter out of suffering, Ghelderode was in great pain long before he turned the whip on himself. Like many another of his characters, he looked toward death as a relief from the endless suffering that is the lot of mankind. The ultimate aim of his "cruelty," unlike that of Artaud, was to draw back the velvet curtains of "society" in order to reveal the deepest of all mysteries – the mystery that has no door.

Chapter Six

Ghelderode, His Critics, and His Audience

To a greater degree than most playwrights in recent memory, Michel de Ghelderode remains, in death as in life, at the mercy of his critics, his drama a "commodity" quite vulnerable to the shifting winds of taste, his reputation truly a hostage to fortune. The pattern of relative "neglect" and "(re)-discovery" that haunted the author's career would continue to repeat itself, albeit in attenuated form, in the three decades after his death, even as a select few of his plays had become more or less permanent additions to the international dramatic canon.

Ghelderode's relative obscurity seems less baffling to some observers than does the sudden burst of publicity and controversy that overtook the playwright during the last 15 years of his life. If, indeed, his contribution to world drama was so significant, why, then, did his plays remain undiscovered for so long and why, once discovered, did they suddenly fall from favor on the Paris stage, only to resurface, during the decades to follow, in such unlikely locations as Eastern Europe and Latin America?

To understand the phenomenon of Acute Ghelderoditis – a term that now seems to have predicted a short-lived phenomenon – it is perhaps useful to review, albeit in relative haste, the recent history of literate or "art" theater in Paris, where actors, directors, and playwrights have always been taken quite seriously indeed. Between 1919 and 1939 – coincidentally (and ironically) the period of Ghelderode's greatest playwriting activity – the art theater in Paris took on a new and vigorous life of its own, thanks in part to infusions of Freudian thought and Pirandellian dramatic theory. By the mid-1930s such major talents as those of Jean Giraudoux (1882-1944) and Jean Anouilh (1910-87) had begun to dominate, transcending the earlier foreign influences with a Gallic wit all their own.

Just ahead, during and after the war, lay the cerebral, argumentative theater of Albert Camus (1913-60) and Jean-Paul Sartre (1905-80). Sartre in particular was to find in the theater a particularly apt vehicle for communicating his otherwise complex ideas, and he soon developed a vivid playwriting style that would draw and hold audiences well into and beyond the 1950s.

Significantly, the Parisian dramatic "horizon" as it developed between world wars allowed little room for "retrospective" experimentation such as Ghelderode's. It was only later, as younger practitioners first began to tire of the "logical" theater that was still enormously popular, that Ghelderode would find his niche, however briefly. It would not be long, of course, before the challenging texts of Adamov, Beckett, and Ionesco arrived to fill the void. In the meantime, Ghelderode's oeuvre, all but complete and most of it already in print, fell more or less readily to hand. Written in flawless French, Ghelderode's texts did not require translation; like those of Jean Genet (1909-86), a lifetime criminal and outcast whose first dramatic efforts were likewise staged in Paris during 1947, Ghelderode's plays offered definite "shock value" along with an intrinsic, instinctive "theatricality" unmatched by most spectacles then being performed in the French capital.

Pending the arrival and reception of Ionesco, not to mention Beckett, Ghelderode's exploration of scenic and dramatic possibilities, together with his graphic contrasts of illusion and reality, helped to point new directions for antirational, "visceral" theater such as that proposed by Antonin Artaud. Genet, a militant homosexual whose plays, like Ghelderode's, tend to stress the prevalence of self-delusion and artifice (albeit from a somewhat different perspective), would thus find his own experiments complemented, and somewhat strengthened, by the simultaneous performance of similarly "antitheatrical" plays that had stood the test of production in Belgium nearly two decades earlier.

Tempting – and accurate – though it might be to link the decline in Ghelderode's theatrical "fortunes" with the rising popularity of Bertolt Brecht in Paris during the 1950s, it is likely also that the prematurely aging Belgian, his productive days well behind him, faced strong competition, at least in the minds of potential directors and performers, from Ionesco and Beckett as well as from Genet. Genet's plays, however convoluted and outrageous, bear witness to ingrained French logic; so too do the plays of Beckett, owing no doubt to the Irishman's lifelong fascination with Cartesian thought processes, often embodied in his characters. What is more, Beckett's morbid preoccupation with death and religion often meets or surpasses Ghelderode's treatment of similar themes, without the taste-straining excess to be found in such Ghelderode efforts as *La Farce des ténébreux* or *Chronicles of Hell*.

In drawing on the folklore of his Flemish heritage, Ghelderode might well have distanced himself permanently from the dramatic tradition suggested by his choice of the French idiom. Before long, playwrights even more "foreign" by birth than Ghelderode would challenge his accomplishments with equally audacious texts likewise composed in French, and the Ghelderode "moment" would have run its course on the Parisian stage. What might also have worked against Ghelderode's assimilation into the French repertory was his evident familiarity with the British tradition, particularly Elizabethan drama and Restoration comedy. In a nation that has traditionally rejected even Shakespeare as "barbaric," Ghelderode would have had to show greater allegiance to France than his masterful command of its language in order for his plays to be granted "permanent residence" in that country.

Outside of France and Belgium, Ghelderode's fame as a dramatist was just reaching its peak at the time of his death in 1962 – the ferment created in France more than a decade earlier having taken that long, in those days, to find its way across the Atlantic and behind the Iron Curtain. Indeed, it was in the Americas and in Eastern Europe that Ghelderode would have his greatest posthumous success, his plays inevitably performed, as by the VVT, in translations prepared without his help. In those parts of the world the aftershock of Acute Ghelderoditis tended to occur at the same time as, or in some cases somewhat later than, the "discovery" of Beckett, Ionesco, Genet, and the early plays of Adamov, who by then had moved off in different, Brechtian directions.

In the United States and Canada, somewhat later in Great Britain, Ghelderode's emergence as a dramatist of worldwide importance owed much to the pioneering work of David Grossvogel, whose 1958 survey of twentieth-century French drama devoted several substantive chapters to "the Belgian current" and particularly to the plays of Ghelderode, on which the American scholar had written and defended his doctoral dissertation at Columbia University some four years earlier. In the concluding chapter of his survey, following a detailed and still authoritative analysis of Ghelderode's plays, Grossvogel called attention to the recent accomplishments of Adamov, Beckett, and Ionesco among the latest developments on the Paris stage, perhaps inadvertently suggesting the aging Belgian as a possible precursor of what Martin Esslin would describe not long thereafter as the Theater of the Absurd. In any event, Ghelderode's initial North American reception owed much to the welcome afforded around the same time to his younger contemporaries writing originally in French.

In the United States and Canada the plays of Beckett and Ionesco had arrived to fill a void not dissimilar to that which had absorbed Ghelderode's efforts in Paris just before and after 1950. Notwithstanding the emergence of such American avant-garde playwrights as Edward Albee (b. 1928), North American actors and directors increasingly turned to Paris in search of inspiration and material, just as they had between the wars. It was not long before the work of Ghelderode, advanced by Grossvogel, began to draw widespread attention, aided in part by translations prepared by George Hauger for the British audience. Soon Ghelderode's plays were being performed by college theater groups throughout the United States and Canada.

Barely 18 months after Ghelderode's death, his work figured prominently in one issue of a major periodical, then known as *Tulane Drama Review*, addressed to theater practitioners and theoreticians. It was in that issue that Lionel Abel, attempting to rebut a generally negative assessment by the late Auréliu Weiss, first described Ghelderode as "our man in the sixteenth century," a label that has adhered to his reputation ever since. More North American productions of Ghelderode would soon follow, as would a spate of doctoral dissertations and master's theses presented at North American universities.

A curious, somewhat unexpected by-product of Ghelderode's North American reception was the publication, in Paris and in French, of no fewer than three book-length monographs originally prepared and defended in American universities as dissertations. Two of them, by Elisabeth Deberdt-Malaquais (1967) and by Jean Decock (1969), would in time contribute to Ghelderode's growing international reputation as "stage people" versed in French sought to learn more about the writer whose plays had caused such a succès de scandale in Paris some two decades earlier. Although both studies provide creditable, perceptive readings of the plays and have spawned several useful articles by others, both remain somewhat "rooted" in the 1960s, if only by the occasional use of existentialist or Absurdist terminology that may well have been misapplied to Ghelderode. Both studies are further hampered by their authors' lack of access to documents later discovered by Roland Beyen – a fact that helps to perpetuate certain errors of fact deriving from the Ostend Interviews.

Thanks in part to the efforts of Decock and Deberdt-Malaquais, as in time to those of Beyen, Ghelderode's plays by the mid-1970s would, like his Christopher Columbus, have circumnavigated the globe, performed as far afield from his native Belgium as Argentina and the Soviet Union. The Columbus play in particular, although hardly the strongest or most representative of Ghelderode's efforts, would prove to be among his more popular "exports," owing no doubt in part to the author's ill-concealed anti-Americanism that radiates throughout the play.

Two international colloquia – in Genoa in 1978 and in Brussels in 1982, the latter marking the twentieth anniversary of Ghelderode's death – would assemble theater scholars and professionals from countries then as remote as Hungary, where the Belgian playwright's reputation was high and rising. His plays had also met with considerable favor in the Scandinavian countries, where their Nordic properties, misunderstood by the Parisian audience, no doubt continued to sound a welcome and familiar note.

As Beyen points out in the introduction to his exhaustive bibliography, Ghelderode's posthumous fortunes tend to fluctuate with regard to both time and place, with certain plays more often performed in certain times and places than others. There will, for example, be Red Magic decades and Pantagleize decades worldwide, while particular national or ethnic groups tend to favor certain Ghelderode plays over others, as shown by the frequency of their performance (see Beyen 1987, xxviii). Germans and Germanic Swiss, for example, show a marked preference for La Balade du grand macabre, while Red Magic remains a perennial favorite in Poland, among the first Eastern bloc countries to discover and perform Ghelderode's plays.

In North America Ghelderode's reputation has proven variable yet generally secure, confined mainly to the academic community. Within a decade after Ghelderode's death, a number of his plays – most notably *Christopher Columbus* and *Chronicles of Hell* had appeared in textbook editions addressed to college students of French. George Hauger's English translations, by then including no fewer than 14 Ghelderode plays, made the author's work accessible to American theater professionals with little or no knowledge of French. The *Tulane Drama Review* issue devoted largely to the recently deceased Belgian playwright would remain in circulation for some time thereafter, inspiring numerous experimental productions both in Hauger's versions and in the original French.

For American spectators and critics, the initial appeal of Ghelderode's plays, like that of Beckett's, lay in their perceived ambiguity, in the "puzzle" surrounding their interpretation. Certain critics, such as Tom Driver and George Wellwarth, saw Ghelderode as a deeply religious playwright, a "Pauline" Christian (the term is Wellwarth's) for whom the behavior of most clerics had proven disappointing. Others, taking Ghelderode's evident anticlericalism at face value, saw him purely as a nihilist. Around the same time, Beckett's bleak portrayals of the human condition in *Waiting for Godot* and *Endgame* would inspire similar speculations concerning the author's religious convictions, which led in turn to further discussion – and to publicity resulting in theatrical production.

Belatedly but perhaps predictably, the greatest posthumous display of interest in Ghelderode's work has occurred in his native Belgium, led and sustained by the indefatigable Roland Beyen, whose painstaking research not only legitimized Ghelderode studies in academic circles but also served, through his participation in the colloquia at Genoa and at Brussels, to promote the worldwide dissemination of Ghelderode's work. By 1982, the year of the second colloquium, Beyen had managed, by sheer industry and dedication, to inscribe himself permanently within the ongoing saga of Ghelderode and his checkered career. As I have noted earlier, Beyen claims not to have planned his life's work but rather to have stumbled into it when, shortly after Ghelderode's death, he undertook the seemingly modest task of studying the plays in chronological order. Discovering not long thereafter the author's ingrained habit of revising his own history to suit him, Beyen was appalled that none of Ghelderode's prior critics had bothered to delve beneath the carefully constructed surface, instead accepting on unfounded faith a number of factual errors perpetuated in the Ostend Interviews and elsewhere. The studies by Decock and by Deberdt-Malaquais, in particular, were shown to be flawed by serious errors of fact and chronology that, in Beyen's view, might well have been avoided by more scrupulous research methods. Not without a touch of arrogance, Beyen would continue, as late as 1987, to demand of others the same rigorous standards that he had set for himself.

As Ghelderode's posthumous reputation began to emerge as a kind of Belgian national treasure, certain of the playwright's friends and admirers would publish "studies" of their own, many of them little more than thinly disguised memoirs and some of them openly critical of the "scientific" method used by Beyen and his students. There have also been, as Beyen recounts, unfortunate "conflicts of succession" between Ghelderode's French-speaking and Dutch-speaking admirers (Beyen 1987, xxxi). Notwithstanding, the Belgians had by 1990 assumed dominance in the study and production of Ghelderode's plays, with a number of live and broadcast performances given yearly in and around Brussels.

Worldwide, critical and practical interest in Ghelderode's work remained sufficiently strong 30 years after his death to suggest significant further activity with the approach of his centennial in 1998. His work, however, continues to repel even as it attracts, and there remains the ingrained "language barrier" – of the Fleming who wrote only in French – that has hampered the reception of his plays from the start. Certain of his plays – *Escurial, Barabbas, Red Magic*, and possibly *Pantagleize* – seem already well-established in the international dramatic canon, while some others, particularly those that occasioned his initial successes in Paris, appear to have fared less well. Ironically, if Ghelderode's reputation owes its success to any single play, that play is probably *Escurial*, written some years before the author had committed himself definitively to the sixteenth-century mode. Unlike most of the later plays, *Escurial* proves, through the intensity of its largely psychological action and the tightness of its construction, that brevity can indeed be the soul of drama as well as of wit.

Although considerably more limited – and self-limiting – than might have been inferred from their initial postwar reception in Paris, Ghelderode's plays continue to suggest possibilities for the stage, a truly open-ended performance in which text, sound, and spectacle combine to bring actors and audience into confrontation with themselves. When well-executed, the best of Ghelderode's plays have few peers in the domain of "total theater," surpassing even the wildest dreams of Artaud. Unfortunately, Ghelderode's total dramatic output remains flawed and uneven, deterring many directors from even attempting to stage his plays. One viable option, already attempted with success on more than one occasion and in several different locations, is the performance of "Ghelderode shows" comprising carefully selected excerpts from several different plays. Another successful option, lying somewhat outside the scope of this study, is that of musical adaptation – as opera, oratorio, or ballet – many of which have been composed and performed in Europe over the years since Ghelderode's death.

Vigorous in the ever-present face of death, lusty and indeed lustful even as it appears to condemn reproduction and the life toward which it tends, Ghelderode's dramaturgy will continue to draw merited attention as long as actors, directors, and potential spectators return to the stage in search of stimuli and inspiration. The deliberately archaic themes and setting of Ghelderode's best plays, never timely, remain timeless in their portrayal of mankind's elemental struggle against the inevitability of death – as, to be sure, of life itself.

Notes and References

Chapter One

1. *Les Entretiens d' Ostende*, ed. R. Iglésis and Alain Trutat (Paris: L'Arche, 1956), 10; hereafter cited in text as *EO*. My translation.

2. Lionel Abel, "Our Man in the Sixteenth Century: Michel de Ghelderode," *Tulane Drama Review* 8, no. 1 (Fall 1963): 62-71.

3. Roland Beyen, *Michel de Ghelderode, ou La Hantise du masque: Essai de biographie critique* (Brussels: Palais des Académies, 1971), 50; hereafter cited in text.

4. Jacqueline Blancart-Cassou, *Le Rire de Michel de Ghelderode* (Paris: Klincksieck, 1987), 34; hereafter cited in text.

5. Jean Stevo, *Office des ténèbres pour Michel de Ghelderode* (Brussels: André de Rache, 1972), 19.

6. Jean Francis, *L'Eternel aujourd'hui de Michel de Ghelderode* (Brussels: Musin, 1968), 99-102; hereafter cited in text. See also Beyen 1971, 101-109.

7. Roland Beyen, *Bibliographie de Michel de Ghelderode* (Brussels: Académie Royale de Langue et de Littérature Françaises, 1987), 47-48.

8. Roland Beyen, *Ghelderode* (Paris: Seghers, 1974), 84-85; hereafter cited in text.

Chapter Two

1. *Le Cavalier bizarre*, in *Michel de Ghelderode, Théâtre*, vol. 2 (Paris: Nouvelle Revue Française-Gallimard,1952), 23. My translation. Plays from the Gallimard editions (vols. 1-6) hereafter cited in text by volume and page number.

2. Jean Decock, *Le Théâtre de Michel de Ghelderode: Une dramaturgie de l'anti-théâtre et de la cruauté* (Paris: Nizet, 1969), 41-43; hereafter cited in text.

Chapter Three

1. *Michel de Ghelderode: Seven Plays*, vol. 2, ed. George Hauger (New York: Hill & Wang, 1964; London: MacGibbon & Kee, 1966), 175; hereafter cited in text as *SP* and volume number.

2. *Michel de Ghelderode: Seven Plays*, vol. 1, ed. George Hauger (New York: Hill & Wang, 1960; London: MacGibbon & Kee, 1961), 51; hereafter cited in text as *SP* and volume number.

Selected Bibliography

PRIMARY WORKS

In French

Plays

Beginning in 1950, Ghelderode's most significant plays were issued in a standard edition by Nouvelle Revue Française-Gallimard in Paris, superseding earlier editions published in Belgium in the 1930s and 1940s. Date and content of each Gallimard volume are as follows:

Vol. 1 (1950): *Hop, Signor!, Escurial, Sire Halewyn, Magie rouge, Mademoiselle Jaire, Fastes d'enfer.*

Vol. 2 (1952): *Le Cavalier bizarre, La Balade du grand macabre, Trois acteurs, un drame, Christophe Colomb, Les Femmes au tombeau, La Farce des ténébreux.*

Vol. 3 (1953): *La Pie sur le gibet, Pantagleize, D'un diable qui prêcha merveilles, Sortie de l'acteur, L'Ecole des bouffons.*

Vol. 4 (1955): *Un soir de pitié, Don Juan, ou Les Amants chimériques, Le Club desmenteurs, Les Vieillards, Marie la misérable, Masques ostendais.*

Vol. 5 (1957): *Le Soleil se couche, Les Aveugles, Barabbas, Le Ménage de Caroline, La Mort du Docteur Faust, Adrien et Jusémina, Piet Bouteille.*

Vol. 6 (1982): *Le Sommeil de la raison, Le Perroquet de Charles-Quint, Le Singulier trépas de Messire Ulenspiegel, La Folie d'Hugo van der Goes, La Grande Tentation de Saint-Antoine, Noyade des songes.*

Le Siège d'Ostende. Brussels: Musin, 1980. According to Roland Beyen, this first publication of Ghelderode's most "notorious" play is severely flawed by misreadings of a holograph manuscript – misreadings that might have been corrected by consulting extant typescripts approved by Ghelderode.

Narrative Prose

L'Homme sous l'uniforme. Brussels: Musin, 1978.

Sortilèges. Paris: Marabout, 1962; Brussels: Antoine, 1982.

English Translations

Escurial. Translated by Ingrid Strominger Gherman. In *An Anthology of
Modern Belgian Theater.* Troy, N.Y.: Whitston, 1982.

Michel de Ghelderode: Seven Plays. Vol. 1. Edited by George Hauger.
New York: Hill & Wang, 1960; London: MacGibbon & Kee, 1961.
Contains *The Women at the Tomb, Barabbas, Three Actors and Their Drama,
Pantagleize, The Blind Men,* and *Chronicles of Hell* (all translated by
Hauger); also *Lord Halewyn* (translated by Gerald Hopkins). Also
contains excerpts from the Ostend Interviews, translated by Hauger.

Michel de Ghelderode: Seven Plays. Vol. 2. Edited by George Hauger. New
York: Hill & Wang, 1964; London: MacGibbon & Kee, 1966. Contains
*Red Magic, Hop, Signor!, The Death of Doctor Faust, Christopher
Columbus, A Night of Pity, Piet Bouteille, Miss Jairus.* Also contains
excerpts from the Ostend Interviews, translated by Hauger.

The Strange Rider and Seven Other Plays. Translated by Samuel Draper.
New York: published privately for the American Friends of Michel de
Ghelderode, 1964. Includes *The Blind Men, The Women at the Tomb,
The Strange Rider, Evening Lament, The Old Men, Red Magic,
Christopher Columbus,* and *Pantagleize.* Not offered for public sale.

SECONDARY WORKS

Beyen, Roland. *Bibliographie de Michel de Ghelderode.* Brussels: Académie
Royale de Langue et de Littérature Françaises, 1987. Comprehensive in
scope and ambition, Beyen's exhaustive bibliography lists more than
6,000 primary and secondary sources, most of which are readily
accessible to scholars.

———. *Ghelderode.* Paris: Seghers, 1974. Contains Beyen's first full
elaboration of his reestablished Ghelderode chronology, together with
useful analyses of what Beyen considers to be the most significant
plays, considered in true chronological order; a concise synthesis of
Ghelderode's plays and their fortunes concludes the volume.

———. *Michel de Ghelderode, ou La Hantise du masque: Essai de
biographie critique.* Brussels: Palais des Académies, 1971. Based on
scrupulous scholarship, Beyen's comprehensive biography covers
nearly all details of Ghelderode's life and career, correcting many
errors perpetuated by the playwright in the Ostend Interviews and
elsewhere. Concluding chapters deal in depth and detail with such
"problem areas" in Ghelderode's life as women, ethnic minorities, and
the Belgian nation.

———, ed. *Michel de Ghelderode, ou La Comedie des apparences.* Paris and
Brussels: Laconti, 1980. This catalog of the Ghelderode exhibit held at
Beaubourg (Centre Pompidou) in Paris in 1980 assembles many
valuable Ghelderode documents.

Blancart-Cassou, Jacqueline. *Le Rire de Michel de Ghelderode*. Paris: Klincksieck, 1987. Firmly grounded in Beyen's meticulous biobibliographic research, this study is the first to treat all of Ghelderode's work, dramatic and nondramatic, in depth and detail, tracing the sources and effects of the author's characteristic "gallows humor."

Deberdt-Malaquais, Elisabeth. *La Quête de l'identité dans le théâtre de Ghelderode*. Paris: Editions Universitaires, 1967. Somewhat dated in its approach, prepared without benefit of Beyen's discoveries, this study is still useful for its "readings" of the major and minor plays and for its perceptive analysis of Ghelderode's principal characters.

Decock, Jean. *Le Théâtre de Michel de Ghelderode: Une dramaturgie de l'anti-théâtre et de la cruauté*. Paris: Nizet, 1969. Based on an American doctoral dissertation defended in 1964, Decock's study situates Ghelderode as a highly independent Flemish precursor of subsequent trends in avant-garde theater. Notable for careful, provocative interpretations of the major plays, Decock's study, like that of Deberdt-Malaquais, was prepared too early to profit from Beyen's research and thus perpetuates certain errors of fact based on the Ostend Interviews.

Driver, Tom F. *Romantic Quest and Modern Query: A History of the Modern Theater*. New York: Dell, 1970. In an exhaustive survey of world drama since Goethe, written from a theological perspective, Driver singles out Ghelderode's drama as "the most authentic and dramatically viable body of religious drama of modern times," helping thus to "build" Ghelderode's reputation in North America.

Francis, Jean. *L'Eternel aujourd'hui de Michel de Ghelderode*. Brussels: Musin, 1968. One of several anecdotal tributes prepared by friends and associates in the decade after Ghelderode's death, this is a useful volume for its insights into the playwright's character and art. Offers memorable biographical detail that, according to Beyen, may or may not be wholly reliable.

Grossvogel, David I. *20th-Century French Drama*. New York: Columbia University Press, 1961. Originally published in 1958 as *The Self-Conscious Stage in Modern French Drama*, Grossvogel's ground-breaking study not only revealed Ghelderode's work to the English-speaking audience but also sought, and found, meaning in the bewildering body of French-language drama from Alfred Jarry and Paul Claudel to Samuel Beckett and Eugène Ionesco. Nearly indispensable in its time as a guide to recent French theater in general, Grossvogel's book is still useful for its lengthy, penetrating analysis of Ghelderode's plays, developed from the author's 1953 doctoral dissertation.

Guicharnaud, Jacques, with June Guicharnaud. *Modern French Theater from Giraudoux to Genet*. 2d ed. New Haven, Conn.: Yale University

Press, 1967. Overview of recent developments in French drama, similar in scope and purpose to Grossvogel's; deals rather cursorily with Ghelderode's plays, all but dismissing them as staged poetry.

Iglésis, R., and Alain Trutat. *Les Entretiens d' Ostende*. Paris: L'Arche, 1956. Interview with the author.

Michel de Ghelderode et le théâtre contemporain. Brussels: Société Internationale des études Michel de Ghelderode, 1980. The proceedings of the first international Ghelderode colloquium in Genoa (1978). Presents a number of perceptive short studies, most notably by Marie Collins on *L'Ecole des bouffons*, Michèle Fabien on *Hop, Signor!*, Hans-Ludwig Scheel and Michel Otten on *Don Juan*. Also contains valuable documentation on Ghelderode's international "fortunes" in Russia, Hungary, and Poland.

Pronko, Leonard Cabell. *Avant-Garde: The Experimental Theater in France*. Berkeley: University of California Press, 1962. Written during the "heyday" of Beckett and Ionesco, this study is notable for its inclusion and "situation" of Ghelderode within the larger context of experimental drama then being performed in France.

Stevo, Jean. *Office des ténèbres pour Michel de Ghelderode*. Brussels: André de Rache, 1972. Similar in aim and spirit to Jean Francis's volume, Stevo's informed, scholarly "tribute" to Ghelderode nevertheless remains among the better short studies of the playwright and his work, with useful chronology and notes.

Trousson, Raymond, ed. *Michel de Ghelderode: Dramaturge et conteur*. Brussels: Editions de l'université de Bruxelles, 1983. The proceedings of the second colloquium in Brussels (1982) to mark the twentieth anniversary of Ghelderode's death; publishes further accounts of the playwright's international "fortunes," together with several articles on his narrative prose (as indicated by the subtitle).

Tulane Drama Review 8, no. 1 (Fall 1963). Roughly half of this issue is devoted to an assessment of Ghelderode's contributions to world drama, with useful articles by Lionel Abel, Samuel Draper, and Auréliu Weiss. George Wellwarth's contribution is essentially an early version of his chapter on Ghelderode in *The Theater of Protest and Paradox*.

Wellwarth, George E. *The Theater of Protest and Paradox: Developments in the Avant-Garde Drama*. New York: New York University Press, 1964. The chapter on Ghelderode, dealing with both major and minor plays, helped to establish the playwright's reputation with and English-speaking audience, particularly among actors and directors. Like Tom F. Driver after him, Wellwarth tends to read and view Ghelderode as a primarily religious playwright, interpreting his plays in the reflected light of "orthodox" Christianity.

Index

The Author

A 1963 graduate of Hamilton College, David B. Parsell received his M.A. and Ph.D. in French language and literature from Vanderbilt University. Having begun his teaching career at Grinnell College, he has served since 1969 on the faculty of Furman University, where he is currently professor of modern languages. Over the years he has contributed extensively to reference works dealing with the twentieth-century drama and fiction, both French and American, and is the author of *Louis Auchincloss* (1988).

The Editor

David O'Connell is professor of foreign languages and chair of the Department of Foreign Languages at Georgia State University. He received his Ph.D. from Princeton University in 1966, where he was a National Woodrow Wilson Fellow, the Bergen Fellow in Romance Languages, and a National Woodrow Wilson Dissertation Fellow. He is the author of *The Teachings of Saint Louis: A Critical Text* (1972), *Les Propos de Saint Louis* (1974), *Louis-Ferdinand Céline* (1976), *The Instructions of Saint Louis: A Critical Text* (1979), and *Michel de Saint Pierre: A Catholic Novelist at the Crossroads* (1990). He is the editor of *Catholic Writers in France since 1945* (1983) and has served as review editor (1977-79) and managing editor (1987-90) of the *French Review*.